Keep Your Laugh On

JENNIFER & PATTY KNOX,
MARGIE MCCREADY

WESTBOW
PRESS®
A DIVISION OF THOMAS NELSON
& ZONDERVAN

All scripture quotations, unless otherwise indicated, are taken from the Holy Bible, New International Version®, NIV®. Copyright ©1973, 1978, 1984, 2011 by Biblica, Inc.™ Used by permission of Zondervan. All rights reserved worldwide. www.zondervan.com The "NIV" and "New International Version" are trademarks registered in the United States Patent and Trademark Office by Biblica, Inc.™

WestBow Press books may be ordered through booksellers or by contacting:

WestBow Press
A Division of Thomas Nelson & Zondervan
1663 Liberty Drive
Bloomington, IN 47403
www.westbowpress.com
1 (866) 928-1240

Because of the dynamic nature of the Internet, any web addresses or links contained in this book may have changed since publication and may no longer be valid. The views expressed in this work are solely those of the author and do not necessarily reflect the views of the publisher, and the publisher hereby disclaims any responsibility for them.

Any people depicted in stock imagery provided by Thinkstock are models, and such images are being used for illustrative purposes only. Certain stock imagery © Thinkstock.

ISBN: 978-1-5127-3344-0 (sc)
ISBN: 978-1-5127-3345-7 (hc)
ISBN: 978-1-5127-3343-3 (e)

Library of Congress Control Number: 2016903670

Print information available on the last page.

WestBow Press rev. date: 3/22/2016

Series Title Page

Other books by these authors:

A humors and heartwarming collection of true life experiences to bring refreshment, laughter, and joy to the weary soul.

Other material by Jennifer Knox:

Complete two year children's ministry curriculum for 1st - 5th grade. Also available in Spanish.

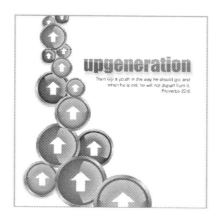

Complete two year children's ministry curriculum for 6th - 12th grade. Also available in Spanish.

If you would like to have Patty, Margie or Jennifer come and speak at your event you can contact us at info@unitednw.org.

Dedication

We dedicate this book to our Lord and Savior Jesus Christ.

Acknowledgment

Thank you to Micah Knox, Sarah Annillo, Kim Cushing and Veronica Rush-Eckhardt for all your hours of work in helping us complete this project. We love and appreciate you all.

Also a huge thank you to United NW Church for supporting us in this project. For more information on United NW Church visit unitednw.org.

Preface

Have you had a crazy week? Dog chewed up the cushion on your new couch? Maybe you just experienced a bad hair cut and color, or like myself, you have been dealing with unruly hair for years! Might be you were brushing your teeth this morning and to your dismay figured out you are truly entering menopause by the five o'clock shadow that suddenly surfaced on your face.

Perhaps you spent a long day at the Zoo and on your trip home you entered the nearest drive-thru to order food for those starving preschoolers. Then you arrive home and quickly realized they short changed you the chicken nuggets. Now, not only do you have whining, hungry kids, but they refuse to eat their fries without their nuggets! And no amount of ketchup coaxing seems to be bringing the desired results you had hoped for. Just when you think things couldn't get any worse, the door bell rings and it is your mother in law. Your house looks like a cyclone blew through it, and on the way to answer the door you discover the new puppy chewed the head off Sally's favorite doll! Sound familiar? No? Well let me toss out a few more. Ever been locked out of your house and ended up on your roof waiting to be rescued? Or gotten stuck in your kitchen window trying to get back in? Ever slip and fall flat on your back covering yourself with the very garbage you were taking out? Ever heard of a kid in school getting a mouth guard appliance stuck in the open position and feeling like a donkey about to bray? I have!

We all have days, weeks and perhaps even months on end when life's intrusions either raise our temperature or just plain bog us down.

This book was birthed from similar experiences. Some serious, many funny, and a few downright hilarious! Margie, Jennifer and myself have all participated in a myriad of life's escapades. We have shared many of these funny adventures at numerous women's events and they were so well received that we decided to compile some of our favorites and pass them on to you. These stories promise to give you a fresh new perspective and keen insight into the ordinary and not so ordinary events of your daily lives, where you can learn to lighten up, find the funny and see for yourself how

God can communicate His love and wisdom through commonplace occurrences.

Finally, rest assured and delight in the fact that Jesus desires to be right smack dab in the middle of our daily lives. And one need only to look at the backside of an Orangutan to be convinced that the good Lord has a great sense of humor! We pray this book, that has come about from our life experiences, will cast a ray of sunshine and encouragement into yours. God is the author of laughter, so go ahead, lighten up and "Keep Your Laugh On!"

- Patty Knox

Biographies

Patty Knox has been married to her husband, Bob, for forty-five years. Together they have four children: Jason, Micah, Nathan and Alison. She is currently the women's pastor of United NW Church where her son Micah and his wife Jennifer pastor. Patty has been blessed with nineteen grandchildren. She can testify to the truth that a merry heart really does good like a medicine, and that a dose of laughter can be the spoon that administers it.

Margie McCready has been married to her husband, Mark, for thirty-six years. She is the mother of five daughters: identical twins Rachel & Melanie, Corinne, Heather and Hillary. Margie also has eleven amazing grandchildren. She's a homebody and a "nester" who loves to tend to her flowers and wild birds. Her passion is reading.

 Jennifer Knox has been married to her childhood sweetheart, Micah, for nineteen years. Together they have four children: Faith, Hope, Grace, and Justice. Jennifer enjoys homeschooling her children and helping with the women and children's ministry of their church, United NW. She's had a passion for Jesus since she was very young, and loves having the opportunity to share that passion with others.

Hairs to Ya

Patty Knox

Song of Solomon 4:1 Your hair is like a flock of goats descending from Mount Gilead.

There was a time when the above scripture brought little comfort to my flock of goats. In fact, when my mind contemplated the visual of black wooly goats streaming down my shoulders it made me want to grab the nearest shears and buzz cut my entire flock! Now, if you happen to be a filly who was blessed with a long silky mane you will not relate to my hair dilemma. Only those who have personally experienced an unruly flock of goat's wool can fully apply the aforementioned scripture.

I would have to say here that my flock and I have butted heads for as far back as I can remember. It didn't matter if I applied hair treatments from my mother's hot iron or endured smelly curl free solutions. The truth is, the moment I walked out into a mist or drizzle, or the wind decided to get sassy on me, my goats morphed into a hideous creation of their own choosing.

My hair quandary surfaced when I was born and sprouted my first tuft and by the time I was three I could have been inducted into the "hair of shame" club. I was an official mop head whose arch enemy was the dreaded hairbrush. Having this tool used on my fleece was like taking a rake to the sticker bushes we had out in the backyard.

It did not take me long to scout out hiding places whenever the hairbrush surfaced, and to my advantage being one of nine kids underfoot, my mother didn't always have the time or energy to sniff me out of hiding. This being said, however, didn't stop my spinster great aunt Jenny from flushing me out when she happened on the scene for a visit.

Now, for some bizarre reason great aunt Jenny was fixated with my hair. Perhaps it was due to the fact that she had never observed wooly goat tufts on a human scalp before. I don't know for sure what the obsession was, but she didn't chase after my other three sisters with the hair brush. And to add insult to injury here, she also had the scent of a hound dog and managed to sniff me out of every hiding place on our forty acre spread!

My dear mother tried to console me after Aunt Jenny's visits by reminding me that poor aunt Jenny had never married nor had any little girls of her own to brush their hair. So I always gave in when she rolled into our driveway and rolled me out of my hideout spots. But after she applied a few short tugs, yanks, and jerks with that hairbrush, I was beginning to think it was providence that dear aunt spinster didn't have any little girls because they would no doubt have been bald at a very young age due to her obsessive compulsive handling of that brush!

I remember retreating to the mirror after she took her leave to assess the damage, and it never failed; my pulsating, throbbing and shaken flock of goats (poor critters) had not only descended from Mount Gilead, but had scattered in every possible direction, leaving in their absence the biggest lion's mane known to the animal kingdom!!!

I thought I had finally found a cure for my unruly flock, when our neighbors had some relatives visiting and a girl about my age with beautiful silk tresses exited the car. I was instantly on a mission to find the secret behind those lovely strands of hair. I quickly invited her over to play. Big mistake! Huge error in judgment. Why you ask? Because underneath that hallowed hair was the bossiest mouth that ever uttered words! If all of us kids wanted to ride bikes, she wanted to swim. If swimming was voted on she tried to veto that vote and ride bikes. And this was the same routine with everything we chose to do. It became a neighborhood nightmare and we were living it. If she hadn't been so bossy and tried to rule the neighborhood I would have already been given the secret to this dictator's hair.

We had finally had enough of her shenanigans. This was our turf and from that moment on we made her life miserable. So miserable in fact, she stayed inside the neighbor's house until the day their car was packed and they were ready to leave Dodge. I watched from the fence as hugs were given and goodbyes were passed around. It was truly a bittersweet moment for me, bitter because I had not been given the secret to beautiful hair, but sweet because she was leaving. Suddenly, bossy Betty spotted me and meandered over to the opposite side of the fence and whispered in my ear the best news a frizz head could ever hope to hear. The secret to a manageable mane!

I don't know which one of the neighborhood kids spilled the beans about my hair, (God bless them) but somehow she got wind of it and spilled her secret! I could not believe my ears. She trotted off from whence she came and was soon heading back to her hometown. About this time I was beginning to feel the pangs of guilt for being so mean to her, but they faded fast when I figured she probably felt guilty for her bossy behavior and that's why she coughed up the secret, so we could call it a truce.

On to the secret of lovely locks. I bolted into Mom's kitchen and emptied the chicken scrap bucket of all the latest potato peelings and scarfed them down. I kept up the regiment of consuming spud peelings for days with no visible change in the goat's tuft. Finally, one morning my mother caught me red handed stealing from the hens and chicks and I had to divulge the secret to radiant hair. I must say, I was not prepared for her reaction. First she looked puzzled, then she laughed so hard she had to use the corner of her apron to dry her eyes.

Seems like I was bamboozled, duped, hoodwinked by bossy Betty. Payback in potato peelings! And to think she had me rustling through that rusty old smelly chicken scrap bucket while she was laughing up her sleeve and stopping for ice cream cones all the way home!

Many years have passed now since great aunt Jenny and the dreaded hairbrush, not to mention the secret to a new 'do. And believe it or not, the goats and I have reached a truce (they let me use the flat iron on them).

Guess I was so focused on looking like everyone else that I couldn't be content with the way God designed me. The bible tells us that God handcrafted us into the unique individuals that we are, mop heads and all, and that it delights Him. Really? Yep, designed by His good pleasure for His good pleasure. Well, that news was sure a lot easier to swallow than potato peelings.

Hmm… maybe someday soon I will retire my flat iron and invest in a hairbrush. You know, go back to my wooly roots and take pleasure in the truth that God adores me - frizz head and all. And if I ever run into bossy Betty again I'll tell her the secret of real contentment.

Each Tooth Must Have Its Twin

Jennifer Knox

Song of Solomon 4:2 Your teeth are like a flock of sheep just shorn, coming up from the washing. Each has its twin; not one of them is alone.

I love the Bible! I really love MY Bible! Ask anyone who knows me, and they would vouch for this. I love the Bible like I love my life. My Bible is well worn and shows memories of Bible studies, personal soul searching, prayers, tears and even laughter. The one thing I hold onto in life, with all its challenges, questions and struggles is this... the Word of God is true!

Knowing that the Bible is true has helped me through many of life's tough decisions, but one that is particularly fresh in my mind is the journey of my tooth! See, loving the Word as I do, I knew the verse in Song of Solomon 4:2 that says, "Your teeth are like a flock of sheep just shorn, coming up from the washing. Each has its twin; not one of them is alone." So when my dentist, a God fearing man, offered up the potential of pulling one of my teeth, I knew he had forgotten that each tooth is like a sheep and must have its twin!

It was a long journey even getting to this point in my life. As I laid on the familiar curvy chair, with the light beaming in my eyes, and my mouth's reflection staring at me from my dentist's glasses, I remembered what brought me to this moment. It was ten years prior that I had a small cavity that needed to be filled. My husband and I were short on finances at the time and so I hunted down the cheapest dentist I could find. Hindsight tells me this was not a good idea! When I walked into the overcrowded waiting room, I realized that I was not the only one to search out the bargain dentist deal of the day.

After a long wait in a dank room, I was ushered to the back area and placed in the traditional curvy chair, the one with the bump at the knee to make you think you will be comfortable laying in it for hours. The dentist informed me that I did have a small cavity on my back top right molar. Within moments I was being shot up with Novocain and prepared for the dreaded filling! I hate fillings! I hate fillings more than I hate almost anything else! I know we should use the word "hate" sparingly, but it is the only word that can accurately describe my true feelings towards this dreadful event! As the dentist finagled the drill to the back of my mouth, he began to speak to his assistant in another language. I'm not sure what language it was, but being the observant type, I assumed it was an Indian dialect. I was hoping they were discussing how to be extra gentle with the patient in their care when all of a sudden I heard a terrible crunch coming from the back of my mouth! The dentist made some sound that resembled, "uh oh!" Now, when your mouth is open to about fifty times its ability and someone has a drill in their hand, "uh oh" is not exactly comforting!

I left the overcrowded office with a numb cheek and a drooping lip, but was glad the whole thing was over... or so I thought! For two weeks I was in constant pain from where I had my "little" filling. After some prodding from others, I went back to the dentist to find out why I was experiencing such pain. This time I had a different dentist look at my tooth and he informed me that the filling had been so deep and close to the nerve, that I may need a root canal! To my complete shock, the first dentist had actually broken my tooth in half! That explained the strange shape my tooth had taken after my first visit. Since I was NOT prepared for a root canal, I chose some medication to help calm the nerve pain. After a month or so, the pain was gone and I grew accustomed to my half tooth.

Ten years would pass before I would go to another dentist, which is about nine years longer than it should have been. When my new dentist (the God fearing one) saw the half tooth, he said I should have it refilled with a porcelain filling. GREAT! Round two! This filling was not nearly as interesting as the first go around, but I did leave with a pretty, WHITE, half tooth. But as the Novocain wore off, the familiar ache was back. The nerve could not handle the trauma. Yes... my dentist even acknowledged it was TRAUMA!

I actually went an entire year with my tooth aching more and more until the day of reckoning came... either the tooth went, or I had to have a root canal! Knowing I had to keep "the twins" together, I chose the latter. The next day I walked into a specialist's office to await the procedure. When the doctor came to get me, he told me not to worry, because I would be given "laughing gas." Laughing gas does have an official name, but to us commoners, it's laughing gas. I had in my mind that it would be a mask over my nose and mouth, but no... this mask just goes over the nose and looks like a pig nose with cords running down both cheeks to keep it balanced. Now, as if it isn't humiliating enough to lay with your mouth ripped wide open, drool being slurped up through a sucker… now I had a pig nose!

The doctor kept asking if I was feeling the results of the gas, but I wasn't. He kept assuring me that I would feel very relaxed and almost sleepy, but I can assure you… I was anything but! My heart was racing and I was hating every moment! I shook my head "no" to him again, letting him know I was feeling NOTHING but fear! It was about that time he got up and walked out of the room. There I was, alone, scared, mouth open and pig nose on! Then the room started spinning, and I mean spinning! Then my ears started making an alarming beeping sound. I had enough mental clarity to actually think to myself, "I didn't know that ears could make this sound!" It was horrible! The beeping, the spinning, then the nausea! I knew if I didn't get the pig mask off, I would be throwing up! I pulled it off and in a moment the world was returning back to normal. I was still dazed when the doctor walked back in and informed me that they had a problem with the gas, and that's what the alarm was for. So… that sound wasn't coming from my ears… it was just an alarm letting them know anyone on the gas might die! Well, I'm not sure that's what the alarm meant, but I do know I got a sudden massive dose of the stuff!

Once it was corrected, I finally started to relax and did feel quiet sleepy. Things were looking up!

It's a strange moment when you find yourself snoring, but you're awake and you don't care. I could hear myself snoring, but I was so comfortable, that I felt no need to stop. This root canal was appearing to be a breeze! That's until I felt another CRUNCH! Then I felt the doctor and his assistant looking for a tool in my hair! I couldn't imagine what had just happened, but then again I didn't really care because I had the pig nose on and life was peaceful.

After a couple hours of snoring while awake, the pig nose came off and I was sat back up. My head was still a little loopy when the doctor informed me that something had happened. I couldn't quite tell what he was saying because my head was so foggy, but it sounded as if he said he had broken a tool in my tooth and was going to leave it there! It was all somewhat confusing as he was assuring me he would not charge to remove whatever it was he was talking about. I quickly brushed off the thought because he moved onto his next point, my cheek! Apparently, ever so rarely the needle for the Novocain nicks a blood vessel and causes swelling and bruising. Well, wouldn't you know... mine was nicked! My cheek was HUGE! Imagine putting an apple in the side of your mouth and leaving it there for a month! That's pretty much what it was, only add to that a nice green and purple hue!

As I was paying my $500 fee at the front desk and holding my chipmunk cheek in my hand, I felt a sharp poke on my neck. What was that? I looked down to see that I had been attacked by a sharp file. The doctor smiled politely at me as I handed it to him. "That's where that went! We looked for it when it broke in your mouth, but we couldn't find it!" I was starting to wonder if there was any deduction from my bill for over gassing, blood vessel nicking and file poking your patient, but apparently there wasn't.

For over a month I tried to cover my very green cheek with make-up and was relieved to finish up the process with a "simple" crown! So there I was again in the curvy chair and mouth wide open. My doctor came in holding my paperwork and said, "The specialist reported to me that he broke a portion of his tool and left it in your tooth… for life!" Did I hear that correctly? Yup! There is forever a file stuck in my tooth, they were quick to inform me that this does happen from time to time and that if ever I start to experience pain from it, they would remove it at no extra charge! But… they would have to drill through the side of my gums to get to it!

I laid my head back in amazement at what all had occurred over what was to be a "little" filling. I had plenty of time to think it over, as this "simple" crown visit took hours! To my complete shock, by the end of this appointment I only had a nub of a tooth left! I couldn't believe it! Where was my tooth? I may have only had half a tooth, but at least I had half! Now I only had a little stump of a tooth! My tongue was very curious, as my husband so aptly puts it! The hygienist informed me that this was the procedure for a crown, you basically remove all but a bit of the tooth, then put a fake tooth over it and call it a crown! There was no preparing for the farewell of my half tooth, without my knowledge it was gone.

We were preparing for a week long camping trip on the day they turned my tooth into a stump. They placed a temporary tooth over stumpy and then told me what to do if it was to come off while we were gone. COME OFF? I was horrified at the thought, but thankfully, this was ONE thing that wouldn't happen. I returned back in a couple weeks and my permanent fake tooth, AKA crown, was put into place. The ordeal was finally over… well, unless I ever experience pain and need some major procedure to pull the file out of my tooth… but at no extra charge!

As I left with my fake tooth thinking how sad that it was no longer a twin, I harbored great resentment to old what's his name doctor that split my tooth in half in the first place! What a lot of trauma he caused! And what a lot of money to spend just to keep a twin, which turned out not to be a twin, but a wanna-be-twin! Then the Lord spoke to me as He so often does, "If you had flossed better in the first place, you wouldn't have needed the 'little' filling." Well, I'm not sure if it was the Lord or my conscience, but either way, it was true.

We can be so quick to blame others for the problems in our life, but we have to take responsibility for our own actions. It was true that Mr. Tooth Breaker had caused me a lot of trouble, but it was also true that if I had taken better care of my teeth, I would never had met Mr. Tooth Breaker or Mr. Cheek Nicker, Over Gasser, Leave A Tool In Your Mouth Doctor. It has encouraged me to look into my own life and look for the little things that can become BIG things if not taken care of. Things like forgiveness, my attitude, my thoughts and my motives. They may seem small now, but they can grow into full blown issues if left unchecked. So, to all of you, I pray that we will guard our lives well, floss often… and may you always have a mouth full of twins!

The Pottery Class

Margie McCready

Isaiah 64:8 We are the clay, you are the potter;
we are all the work of your hand.

When I was twenty years old my girlfriend talked me into taking a pottery class. It was not an easy feat. I do not have an artistic bone in my body. She, on the other hand, is amazing. Everything she touches has an artistic flare to it. I finally gave in to her request when I realized I could at least spend quality time with her as we would be doing this together.

The morning of the class it was windy and rainy and I was dreading leaving my cozy house. As we settled at the table, in front of each of us was a big lump of clay. I could not imagine fashioning anything with that clay but I tried to keep an open mind. As the teacher shared her passion as a full fledged potter I gazed around the room. Her creations were everywhere. They were really beautiful. "I can do this," I thought. After working with my clay for quite some time, I realized there must be a secret to this art and no one had shared it with me. The teacher noticed my frustration and suggested I make a simple bowl. Simple bowl? Who was she kidding!! I fought with that clay for an hour and I did end up with a bowl looking thing but it was lopsided and pathetic. I was humiliated and didn't know whether to laugh or cry. My teacher then suggested I remake it. "Remake it?" I said. She then informed me the more I worked with the clay the easier it would become for me to make the bowl. As I glanced across the table I looked at my girlfriend's simple bowl and it was perfect. I wanted to choke her. My bowl looked like a preschooler had made it. I decided to do exactly as the teacher suggested and kept reworking my clay. I finally had my bowl. It did not turn out as well as I would have liked it to, but for me it was acceptable. Making the bowl was a struggle, but I did enjoy painting it. The teacher instructed the class to leave the bowls for her to fire in the kiln, and that we would see the finished products at the next class.

I was not expecting to see much of a transformation upon my return to class, but I was absolutely shocked! I could not believe it was the same bowl. My dull looking bowl with the many visible flaws was beautiful. The flaws were no longer noticeable and the colors were striking. To me, it was a miracle!

I can't help but reflect on the analogy of God being the potter and we being the clay. If we will yield ourselves to Him, He will shape our lives into something beautiful. He is patient and kind and His touch on our lives is always gentle and loving. Since God is the Potter and the Shaper of our lives we must acknowledge his sovereignty over us. It is He who formed us out of the dust and it is He alone who reserves the right to mold us into vessels fit for His kingdom. It was in the fire that the true colors of the clay were brought out and the same is true for us. Some of God's very best work is done in the "furnace times" of our lives.

It is where He tempers us and brings out the true colors of His character in us. I learned to love the pottery class and made some very special items that I have passed down to my children. I will never be a great potter but I belong to the greatest Potter ever.

God is My Personal Trainer

Jennifer Knox

1 Timothy 4:8 For physical training is of some value, but godliness has value for all things, holding promise for both the present life and the life to come.

I've decided that I am an athlete. For me, it all started on my sister's fortieth birthday when she ran a marathon on top of a mountain range! It's a once a year challenge that is done in Montana on the Bridger Mountain Range. These diehard athletes have decided a normal marathon on normal paved roads is no challenge. They have chosen the "narrow" way, by doing what is aptly named The Ridge Run. Yup! They actually run along the ridge of the mountain range.

Since I am related to my athletic sister, I assume I have the same genetic make up and am also an athlete (may I also mention, I am four years younger than her). The first thing I did was set out to buy some good, solid tennis shoes. I'm not talking the cute ones, I'm talking the athlete's shoe of choice. My husband took me as I tried on pair after pair. I bounced, walked, hopped and squatted to make sure I got the perfect ones.

I left the store that day with not one, but two pairs of all terrain running shoes. Now that the shopping was done, it was time for the fun to start. Since there were no mountain ranges near my house for me to run, I decided to start by walking around my neighborhood. Being an athlete is much harder than it appears. By the second day of my jaunt around the block, my legs were telling me I was more of a cheerleader than a runner. By cheerleader, I mean the person who stands on the sidelines and cheers as the marathon runners go by.

It's been several months now that I have been training to venture out of my neighborhood and walk the hill that I live on. I strapped on my super, athletic running shoes (even though I only ever walk), put the head phones on, pumped up the worship music and off I went. The way down was fabulous, the way up was miserable. The entire time I was fighting the urge to quit, but I didn't see any other athletes on the hill stopping, so I pressed on.

The thought came to me on one of my hill treks that God is my personal trainer. I constantly hear people talking about trusting God for everything. I have longed to experience healing from a very difficult time in my life, but the healing hasn't come. I've wanted to trust God to direct me in the way to go, but I never could trust what he would ask of my broken spirit. So, I traipsed through life the best I knew how.

Then it hit me, if I had hired a personal trainer to help me prepare for a marathon along a mountain range, he would never give me step one: go run 32 miles! He would start slow and pace me accordingly. He would know that I didn't have the stamina to do now what I wanted to accomplish later, it would be a process.

How much more our heavenly Father? I could feel my heart opening up to trust Him with the next step I needed to take. He is faithful and good. He wants to see us complete our race and win the prize! He wouldn't look at me and say, "forgive, forget, move on and be perfect right now!" No, He would lead me gently in the way of healing, showing me one small step at a time.

So, not only am I an athlete, I will one day be a healed and healthy athlete! How about you? Do you have a hurt that you just can't seem to hurdle? How about sharing my personal trainer? He is just that... personal. He will create a plan that is perfect for just you.

Time to Grow Up

Margie McCready

Hebrews 6:1 Therefore let us move beyond the elementary teachings about Christ and be taken forward to maturity...

It isn't easy growing up. I remember as a child having my share of challenges as I tried to maneuver my way into adulthood. I also remember being told to "grow up". I didn't like to hear it at the time, but the truth is, I needed to hear it. As painful as it was, it did help me to redirect my thinking and ultimately change my actions.

What applies in the natural life is also relevant in the spiritual life.

As Christians, our walk with the Lord will be stunted if we choose to not get out of the playpen and grow up. Playpens are essential for a time, but if left in them continually, a baby will never learn to walk. The same is true for us. It is in our daily walking with the

Lord that we grow and are changed into His image. It is the walk of maturity.

I have a sister who loved her bottles of milk. She loved them so much that she did not want to give them up and was still drinking them at 4 years old. My mother knew the bottles had to go since my sister would not develop properly without solid food. My sister would soon be starting school, and school is not for babies. Neither is Christianity.

Every single day we should be feeding on His word and growing in our walk with the Lord. Growing up doesn't just happen; it takes effort, diligence and time. We can't stay in the playpen being milk-fed Christians. The Lord desires for us to grow up and "into Him". He wants to grow us into a healthy tree that is planted by the water and produces lush fruit in due season; a tree that has deep roots in Him. If we will choose to grow up and get out of the playpen, then growth will be our reward. We will learn how to discern right from wrong, how to make wise choices and we will be able to apply what we learn to our daily walk with the Lord. The Lord's goal for us is to "Grow Up". Ephesians 5:10 says, "find out what pleases the Lord".

Strive for growth, not perfection.

Oreo Cookies, Toothpaste and Cortaid Ointment... Recipe for Disaster

Patty Knox

Proverbs 26:27 Whoever digs a pit will fall into it; if someone rolls a stone, it will roll back on them.

A few years ago, my husband Bob and I hosted a weekly Bible study in our home. We had several couples in attendance and began an overview of the Old Testament. When we got to the book of Proverbs, I thought it would be a great idea to have everyone make up their own proverb and share it with the group. Little did I know that this would be a prophetic occasion of my undoing!

Before I lead into my story I need to explain something about my better half. Most people that know Bob see him as a man of great faith with Godly character and a passion to pray. As his wife of many years I can most certainly attest to these facts. However, Bob possesses another trait that most aren't privy to. He also has a trickster and jester side.

He loves to play pranks on unsuspecting souls. Allow me to give you a quick example. One afternoon my daughter-in-law, Jennifer, and I were having a leisurely visit in my family room. Bob made an entrance and asked if we would like a root beer float. This kind gesture was graciously received and being moved by his kindness we waited anxiously for our treat to be delivered to us. When it was, Mr. Nice Guy served us up two glasses foaming over the top with pop and stuffed inside with vanilla ice cream. We thanked him several times for his kindness before he exited the room.

Now, as we began to suck the yummy foam from the rim of our glasses, my tongue got a taste of the ice cream below. Hmm, was it just my taste buds or was there an odd taste? I glanced over at Jennifer and noticed that she had an "odd taste" look on her face also. I scooped a spoonful of the stuff and placed it in my mouth only to have my suspicion confirmed. Jen was tracking right along side me here by sniffing the contents of hers.

Mr. Kind Deed just happened to re-enter the room right about this time and inquired as to how it tasted. Being his daughter-in-law and not wanting to offend, Jennifer fibbed for us both and said they were great when in all truth they were awful!!!!! He watched us suffer through a few more bites and swallows and then let out in a guffaw that only stopped long enough to wipe the tears from his eyes.

It seems Bob was going to make himself a root beer float, but when he saw that the ice cream had melted and refrozen leaving that sticky yucky taste, he decided instead to play a practical joke on us and he did indeed!

Back to the Bible study. Remember the Proverb assignment? Just before starting the class I decided to get even with my hubby and took an Oreo cookie that we were going to be snacking on that evening and emptied the middle of its frosting and replaced it with toothpaste. Bob fell for the trick hook, line and sinker. The group watched in anticipation as he smacked his lips after the first bite and when he bit into his second we could barely hold back our laughter. Finally, he remarked to crowd that they must be putting mint in their cookies now. We all had a knee-slapper on that joke and Bob was a good sport, too.

His proverb that night just happened to be along the lines of 'when you trick others you may find yourself tricked instead'. We enjoyed this immensely figuring that proverb sure came to pass. Until the following morning when I grabbed the toothpaste to brush my teeth and suddenly realized by my foaming mouth and numbing tongue that I had somehow grabbed the Cortaid ointment instead. I had forgotten the night before to place the toothpaste back on the shelf after filling Bob's cookie.

Now my husband was the one to have the last laugh while his proverb became two fold for me. Not only had I put my foot in my mouth, but had pulled it out long enough to squirt some numbing ointment in also!

My jokester ways are over concerning Bob. I've nixed all thoughts of getting him back. And I warn you, if he pulls any shenanigans your way, don't try any antics of your own to repay him because I think he and the Lord are in cahoots together.

There are plenty of scriptures in the book of proverbs in the Bible that speak about setting traps for others and the folly of it. I know first hand what they are talking about. Bob on the other hand? His turn will most likely come, but not from me!

Marching to the Beat of a Different Drum "Key"

Jennifer Knox

Proverbs 11:2 When pride comes, then comes disgrace, but with humility comes wisdom.

Very few things can get me out of the house without flat ironing my hair first. I can hardly remember a moment when it has happened since the beloved flat iron entered my life. But this day was special and called for a quick jaunt out sporting my "natural" 'do! For those who have not witnessed it, and sadly there are those who have had to see it, it is best described as... BIG! I believe I have a lineage tied back to the Chia Pet, it's unconfirmed, but quite likely.

My good friend was going to her new home for its inspection before the loan would go through. She had called me and informed me that if I wanted a "pre-purchase peek" at the home, I would have to come over right away. The real estate agent and the house inspector were both there when I arrived. I had not anticipated seeing anyone except my friend, so I was immediately a little off my A game. I was overcompensating for my no make-up, chia pet hair by acting like I knew pretty much everything about houses... when I really knew nothing!

I felt like my "here to answer any of your questions" approach was going fairly well, and I was successfully drawing attention away from my hair. That was until the inspector announced that there was no key to check the gas shut off near the fire place. Being that I was now a walking encyclopedia of answers for all who needed help, I offered to run home and grab mine.

I had been living in my house for about seven years at this point and had faithfully kept the key on the mantel, just as any responsible homeowner would. Since I found the key unsightly, I always kept it hidden behind a vase, but faithfully dusted under it for over half a decade. When I got home, there was my key, just as it always was.

I quickly got back to my friend's house and handed over the key. Chia Pet had just saved the day! To my dismay, though, the inspector and the realtor both informed me that this was NOT a gas shut off key, but a drum key! A drum key? We don't have any drums! AND I have kept careful watch over this key for the past seven years!

A bit perturbed, I stood my ground and informed them that it was most definitely a gas key. I was relieved that my friend sided with Chia Pet woman on this one. I pressed my point with the two insistent men that the houses in my neighborhood must use a different type of key. To which they commented, they had never seen a gas key like this. One of them even said they were a drummer and this was in fact a drum key! I was unmoved, but starting to hear the Chia Pet jingle in my head... "Chi, Chi, Chi, Chia!" I felt the need to get back home and away from onlookers right away.

I grabbed my gas key and headed back home. Immediately I walked over to our emergency gas shut off to put the final blow on their ridiculous theory, when to my dismay... it was about five times too small! I could feel the blood rushing to my face as I replayed my adamant objections to the drum key theory. Where did this ridiculous thing come from! And why have I been coddling it for years! And why did I leave the house with a Chia Head! It just made the whole thing so much more humiliating!

I made the shameful admission to my friend and she enjoyed a great laugh at my expense and soon showed up at my door with a REAL gas shut off key. That key now sits on my mantel where Mr. Drum Key sat for so long.

The whole thing got me thinking about pride. What an ugly item to put on in the morning. I had dressed myself from head to toe in it that day and the results were anything but pretty. However, when we can come to the Lord and admit our weaknesses, our insufficiencies, our insecurities, and the fact that we don't know the difference between a gas key and a drum key... He clothes us with grace, and that is truly beautiful (even if you are a Chia Head)!

Created in the Image of God

Patty Knox

I Corinthians 13:12 For now we see only a reflection as in a mirror; then we shall see face to face.

Visiting some friends, Bob and I had a firsthand experience with distorted images. Our friends could tweak their bathroom mirror in such a way that it changed the image of our faces. Some were hilarious, while others were brutal to behold. It all just depended on the angle of the mirror you happen to be looking through.

Isn't it amazing how life's circumstances can distort and blur the image we see of ourselves when we gaze in a mirror? As little girls, we loved the Cinderella story and had no problem with the Prince rescuing and taking us to the palace to be his Princess. When we looked into the mirror, we saw a maiden worthy to be loved and protected. We felt secure knowing that we were chosen among all the thousands to sit at his side in the Royal Court of his vast kingdom.

Then life's disappointments and heartaches that we never bargained for began to tweak the image of our reflection. Disapproval, rejection and offenses start to fog our mirrors into a misshapen form. For some, betrayal, divorce, and insecurity begin to warp and falsify our true sense of identity.

Perhaps we have been responsible for some of the cracks in our own mirrors, and believe the image reflected back at us is really who we deserve to be. Condemnation and shame cloud our appearance, making it impossible to see any image at all. It's only when we receive forgiveness, forgive ourselves and forgive others that the fog lifts. This life is full of painful circumstances that Satan would love to see rob us from seeing clearly who we were designed to be.

I remember as a little girl starting out believing I was special when I peeked in the mirror (missing teeth and all). But I soon learned that being spurned as a young child by the one who was supposed to rescue me, left me deformed in my mirrored image of myself. I hated looking into any reflection because it reminded me that I was stupid and ugly and not worthy to be loved or accepted. Rejection from someone who has great impact in our lives, I believe, is one of the greatest image robbers, because they have the power to angle the mirror in directions that cause us great harm in seeing ourselves differently than who we are in God's sight.

I'm so thankful that the Bible mirrors for us what our true image looks like. On the sixth day of creation God said, (Genesis 1:26) "Let us make mankind in our image, in our likeness." I don't know about you, but this comforts me immensely. That means every false image that has appeared in our mirrors are counterfeits of what we were designed to be like!

The dictionary defines image as the form in which one appears. It speaks of quality and likeness, resembling someone or something. So how are we made in God's image? Obviously it is not in any physical form, because He has no physical attributes. It means we are to mirror Him in character, to allow His love, mercy, kindness, forgiveness, patience and joy to reside within our hearts and be reflected. I don't think there is a more radiant reflection than that of a human heart given completely to the Lord. This beauty is not based on physical attractiveness or personal achievements. It has nothing to do with human ability and skill. And the really great news is that our value and worth is not measured by others.

There is a prince today that is still rescuing his princesses... He's called the "Prince of Peace" and if we will choose to follow Him, we will see the true reflection of what we were intended to look like... oh yes, there will be days when the mirror seems cloudy because we face difficulties and heartache in this life. But never lose sight of the fact that some day we shall see everything in perfect clarity.... may we seek to reflect the One whose image and likeness we bear.

Mortified

Jennifer Knox

*Hebrews 10:22 Let us draw near to God with a
sincere heart in full assurance of faith, having
our hearts sprinkled to cleanse us from a guilty
conscience and having our bodies washed with
pure water.*

It was one of the highlights of every year, my visit to
see my grandparents. Each summer my cousin Debbie
and I would head to beautiful La Jolla, California to
spend a couple weeks of absolute fun with two of my
favorite people. My grandfather was an orthopedic
surgeon and my grandmother was the perfect high
society wife.

I loved the arrival to their house. It always followed
the same tradition from year to year. We arrived off the
plane to be greeted with hugs and kisses, then straight
to Baskin Robbins for ice-cream. From there, we went
to the house to get settled in. Ahhh, the smell of the

patio as we would come in from the garage carrying our suitcases. We were met with the fragrance of jasmine, orange trees and the distant smell of the ocean saltwater. Staying there was a piece of heaven, however we were never to forget to be on our best behavior!

To spend a vacation with my grandparents was a walk down pampering lane. We dined at the fanciest restaurants, shopped for clothes at high end stores with personal shopping assistants and even once got to be picked up in a limousine for a day at the Ritz Carlton Hotel. At no point though, were we ever to forget our manners! We sat up straight while eating, always waiting for my grandmother to take the first bite before we could eat. We greeted their guests with courtesy. Never complained, even when we had sunburns so bad they blistered (one never put their misery on another... well, at least when in La Jolla). Everything was to be done in a very proper, respectable way.

My cousin and I had mastered the protocol of our visits, as long as you knew how to play the game... it was always fun. Well, on this particular year my cousin had just turned 16 and my grandparents had decided we could take the car and do some of our traditional sightseeing without them. Our first stop... Seaworld!

To anyone who has never been to Seaworld, it is just that, the size of a world, at least the parking lot is. It is not uncommon to have to take a tram to get from your car to the front gate. However, on this particular day we got the pot of gold at the end of the rainbow... a spot right up front! We couldn't believe it! The whole lot was full and we just happened to get this amazing parking spot. When we got out of the car, we saw that it was not only right up front, but shaded by a tree. We were amazed at how loud the tree was, it must have had 100 birds squawking away in it. We marveled at just how many birds could fit in such a small tree. No more thought was given to our parking spot, the tree, or the birds, it was time to see Shamu!

After a very long and fun day we headed back to our car as the sun was setting. Delighted, we didn't have a long walk back, we were surprised to see our once blue car looked peculiarly white! Was this our car? Had someone dropped paint all over it? To our horror it wasn't paint, but a full day parked under a hundred birds. They had left our car covered... and I do mean covered in bird droppings! It was so thick that my cousin had to turn on the wipers and washer fluid just to see out the windshield! I had never seen anything like it. Since I was the passenger, I took the opportunity to humiliate my chauffeur as she drove out of the parking lot. I put my seat all the way back so all you could see was her driving and let me tell you... everyone was looking!

It was late by the time we got home so my grandparents were already in bed. We didn't give another thought to our car issue until the next morning when we got up for breakfast. My grandmother was a devout Catholic and attended mass almost every morning, always going and returning home before we were even up. This morning had been no different, with one exception... the car!

As we sleepily walked into the family room, we were greeted by my grandmother saying, "Girls! What happened to the car?! I was MORTIFIED!!!" She told us she had driven that car all the way through La Jolla to mass and back with one hand on the wheel and the other hand shielding her face from all the people staring! We laughed so hard at the thought of my ever so proper grandmother driving that poop covered car through town!

She made us go with her to the car wash and all three of us were red faced as we pulled up. The guys doing the washing were in total shock as they informed us they had never seen anything even close to this. It had to go through the car wash two times and still be hand washed to get it totally cleaned. After the ordeal was over we were instructed to avoid shady parking spots.

You know, our lives aren't much different from my grandmother's car. We sometimes make choices in our lives that leave us covered with the dirt of sin. We feel ashamed to even face people and our self worth is nowhere to be found. That is when we need to remember we have a heavenly Father who is always ready to send us through the car wash... even twice if we need it and then gently wipe us clean. All of us have sinned and fallen short of the glory of God, but we all have the same opportunity to be washed clean. How good it feels to allow our shame to be removed and the glow of the Holy Spirit to shine through us again!

The Joy of the Lord

Jennifer Knox

Nehemiah 8:10 Do not grieve, for the joy of the Lord is your strength.

Laughing is one of my favorite things to do, it just feels so good! I love those moments when you are sitting around with friends and family and everyone is wiping tears and holding their stomachs from laughing so hard. Unfortunately, we can be misled into thinking that this is what "joy" is. This is laughter, not to be confused with joy.

This truth became clear to me on the day when I saw laughter leave my mother and be replaced with the sting of death. It was February 8th, 1999. I had been awakened to the strange sound of the phone ringing and my grandmother's voice on the answering machine. As I staggered to the phone in a sleepy daze, I wondered, why was my grandmother calling me at 5:00 in the morning? And what was she saying about

Bill? Papa Bill is how we better knew him, he was my mom's husband and my step-dad.

Papa Bill came into our lives at a very dark time for my family. My parents had divorced in a painful and sad ending to a 16 year marriage. My dad remained in Seattle and my mom, my sister and I moved to Atlanta, Georgia to begin a new life. The adjustment was hard and we all felt the sad effects of a family torn apart. Then enters our love... Papa Bill.

He was ten years my mom's senior and so handsome and soft spoken. He immediately captured all of our hearts. He began to fill a lonely place in my heart that only a dad can hold. He brought happiness back into our little home and healing to our broken hearts. Everyone who knew Bill, loved Bill.

My mom and Bill had been married for eight years when they took what was to be their last vacation together. They set off to Florida for a quick trip that was to take a very sad turn. In the hotel the first night, Bill began to experience a severe migraine and eventually he was unable to even stand. An ambulance was called and he was rushed to a nearby hospital with my mom in tow. She was informed there that it was just a migraine headache and that she should go back to her hotel room and come back in the morning. She was only back in her room for a short time when she received the call that her husband had just suffered a stroke and to come at once.

By the time she arrived, he was already on life support, and would not survive. Our beloved Papa Bill was gone. The pain I felt was like nothing I had ever known, it was dark and empty, but nothing to the pain that awaited my mom. Now she was left a widow at the age of 45. She would return from Florida to her home... alone.

My family was on a plane the next day heading to Georgia to bury my step-dad. My head reeled in a fog and the loss was like billowing waves of pain. When we finally got to my parent's house, I couldn't believe how wonderful my mom looked. She was amazingly beautiful! Her eyes were glassy from crying, but her smile shone the entire day. Her strength was astounding, she continued to talk about the glorious day when they would meet again in Heaven. She often quoted Micah's words "Rush me to heaven." It was a play on words, since their last name was Rush.

The day of the funeral arrived and we were led in a long procession to the church behind the hearse that carried our beloved Papa Bill. The guests were all seated in the large, Baptist church that my parents had attended for years. As family members, we were instructed to stay in the foyer until the service was to start. When the moment came, the music started and the casket was ushered down the aisle with my mom behind it. It was then that she broke. This woman who had been so strong and encouraged so many, finally collapsed with grief. She fell to the ground sobbing.

Several people rushed to help her back up, but she just continued to cry with her head pressed against the ground. I could hear her sobs and they were like daggers to my heart. My beloved mom was in so much pain, and there was nothing any of us could do to help her. As the moments passed, she gathered her strength and allowed two people to help her make her way to the front row. She sat in a daze as the preacher spoke about Bill, Heaven, and the goodness of God.

And then it turned. It was the portion of the service when a special guest was asked to sing a worship song. Everyone rose from their seats as the music began. All eyes were firmly on my mom as she lifted herself up from her chair. She then proceeded to walk to the casket and set one hand on the top of it and the other in the air as she worshiped her Lord and Savior.

Here was a woman who just moments before was unable to stand and now she was not only standing, but with hands lifted, was worshiping. What had happened? She had found her joy. See, our joy is not ultimately found on this earth, but in the Lord.

The passage that is so often quoted from the book of Nehemiah is "The joy of the Lord is your strength." Many of us are under the presumption that this means if we have joy, we have strength. However, that is not in the context of this passage. See, the Jews had just returned from being captive in Babylon for over 70 years and now returned to their beloved land of Jerusalem.

Upon their return, Ezra stood up among them and began to read from the Word of God. As the people heard it they were overwhelmed and began to cry with deep cries of regret and remorse! They had not known the word of God prior to this. They had not known how outside His will they had drifted, and now they were hearing the truth of His word and it pierced them to the core.

Seeing the tears and sorrow, Ezra made the comment that they were to take heart, "for the joy of the Lord was their strength!" In the midst of their sorrow comes this amazing word of encouragement that they were not to be sorrowful anymore, for they had once again found the Lord!

Many people say things like, "My kids are my joy." "My husband is my joy." "My job, ministry, money, home, whatever it may be, is my joy." Sadly, all these things can be gone in a moment, only the Lord remains forever.

When my mom's eyes were on her circumstances, she could not even find the strength to stand. But when her eyes looked to her true source of joy, she not only stood, she stood strong! It is my prayer for you that you would know that having the Lord is our true source of joy. We may not be laughing, but we can have joy. We may be weeping, but we still have joy. We may have suffered great loss, but we can NEVER lose our joy if... it is in having the Lord.

Hebrews 12:2-3 says, "Fixing our eyes on Jesus, the pioneer and perfecter of faith. For the joy set before him he endured the cross, scorning its shame, and sat down at the right hand of the throne of God. Consider him who endured such opposition from sinners, so that you will not grow weary and lose heart."

Peggy Sue

Patty Knox

Philippians 3:2a Watch out for those Dogs.

I can still remember the day Peggy Sue joined our family. She was a cute little puppy that my husband Bob, and son Nathan brought home from a box outside a grocery store. Word of caution here. Beware of free puppies. You don't know their breed. We figured out Peggy Sue was part Lab, part Springer Spaniel, and the rest was "Bull Headed."

She never outgrew her need to dig, nor her need to chew. She gnawed through electrical cords, fences, and countless pairs of shoes that the kids left outside. Peggy Sue and I formed a love-hate relationship. She loved to annoy me, and I hated it! That mutt would lay docile at my feet while I hung towels on the clothesline. But the minute I went in to the house to fetch myself a cup of coffee, Peg would fetch herself some towels. Now, she had a strong aversion to commands (due to the bull headedness in her genes). In fact, she never did bow down to any kind of authority, she took it as a challenge. So, racing outside to retrieve my downed towels only set Peggy Sue hot footing it in and out of the bushes, dragging her token of victory through the dirt and beauty bark. Let me enlighten you on this. There is no beauty on a wet towel with bark. I really thought I saw signs of her changing in this area as she got old with joint problems, but she never missed an opportunity to prove me wrong.

If the gate was left open and miss "Bull Headed" got out, it took all the whole neighborhood intervening just to round her up and bring her back. But during the round-up process, she managed to roll in every pile of discarded animal waste matter that she could find. Now this would be annoying to any dog owner, but Peggy Sue had long matted fur. Try cleaning that up....I did learn the trick to getting her back into the gate however. I rewarded her instead of scolding her. It worked every time. She escaped and I fetched the box of doggie treats and gave it a loud shake. The neighbor lady next door disagreed with my method of punishment, but she wasn't privy to Peg's thinking.

Bathing and haircuts for that Dog were grueling for both of us. Why the responsibility always fell in my lap I'll never know. Maybe because no one else would touch her, but trimming that canine was like pulling teeth. Talk about yanks and tugs! One time, I had had it with the scissors and went for the big guns...Hubby's electric razor. It worked wonders on Peggy Sue and gave her a completely new look. Bob agreed when he came home and saw the transformation, until he realized it was his razor that had caused the makeover! (So much for the dog being man's best friend, huh?)

Yep, that Pooch probably put more gray hairs on my head than my own children did. Now I know why God waited until the sixth day to create the animals. If he would have made them sooner, who knows what kind of havoc they would have caused before man came on the scene.

Oh, I loved that bull headed dog if the truth be known. She had her good qualities. She was a great watch dog, and even saved me from a Possum once. She was the first one to greet me when I went outside and the last one to usher me inside. She loved hanging around me, and followed me wherever my boots and shovel took us. I cried the day Peggy Sue was laid to rest. I had experienced what true friendship really looks like. It isn't always walking hand and paw down rose petal paths, some days it's like towels being drug through the bark. It's not always sweet smelling, either.

Sometimes, we and our best friend both have stinky moments. But when we overlook the faults and appreciate the company and faithfulness of a friend who is always glad to greet us with open paws, then I'm figuring it's worth all the drama. I'm glad Peggy Sue showed up at my door. She was good for me. God must have thought so too. In Genesis Chapter one and verse twenty-five, it states, God made all sorts of wild animals (that's my Peg), livestock, and small animals (that fit her description too) to produce offspring of the same kind. And God saw that it was GOOD!....Oh, by the way, I'm happy to report that Peggy Sue got married and had nine little offspring of her own. How many took after her kind? I shudder just pondering the thought.... Thanks Peggy Sue for the friendship and the memories galore!!!!!

The Parable of the Sunflowers

Margie McCready

Matthew 13:23 But the seed falling on good soil refers to someone who hears the word and understands it.

When our twin daughters were teenagers my husband and I decided to volunteer in the youth program at our church. The current youth leader had moved on and because our church also housed a Christian school it was crucial to fill the vacancy as soon as possible. We didn't have a clue at the time what we were getting ourselves into.

We learned early on that the most effective tool for ministering to these young people were object lessons. Jesus used object lessons or parables as He called them because they were very effective. A parable is simply taking a familiar object and putting a different spin on it. It is a great way to teach spiritual truths. The listener must use their own imagination to discover the truth being taught.

One particular Thursday evening I was scrambling to get all my things for youth group together. My day had been very chaotic. As I bolted out the door I realized I had forgotten to prepare an object lesson. I glanced at the fence as I was walking to my car and instantly found my object lesson. Standing side by side were two sunflowers that had been planted at the exact same time. One was four feet tall and stood on a very sturdy stalk with a huge head and beautiful golden color. The other one was stunted and very scraggly. It was half the size of the other one and looked malnourished. The only difference between these two plants was the soil they were planted in. I had run out of my good potting soil when I got to the last panel of the fence. The healthy plant had been planted in the good soil. The scraggly one in the "not so good" soil. The contrast was shockingly apparent. When it comes to planting seeds, soil does matter.

I hurriedly grabbed the two plants and began pulling them out of the ground. The stunted one came out very easily without much effort. The healthy one required some serious maneuvering as its roots had grown much deeper. I had my message that night. I talked to the young people about the soil of their hearts. Jesus spoke about the four soils in the gospels and I tied that into my message. It was very effective. I had the kids come up and handle and inspect the plants. One even asked to take them home. I thanked the Lord for providing me with such a powerful object lesson that night.

Mark and I led the youth group for five wonderful years. It was some of the most rewarding years of my life. I love teenagers because they wear their hearts on their sleeves and they are very transparent. They just want adults to accept them and love them. We have kept in contact over the years with some of our young people. Others have drifted off into the sunset and our paths have never crossed again. Some of the kids took the parable of the sunflowers seriously and cultivated good soil in their hearts. Others did not. One is currently serving a life sentence for attacking two police officers with a knife. Fortunately, there are more good reports than bad.

One of our young men is currently traveling with the mercy ships and helping perform surgeries in other countries. We get a newsletter every month showing the miraculous transformations of people with horrific deformities being corrected and tumors that are being removed. One of our young ladies has been doing missionary work in Thailand, working alongside a pastor there. Two of our young men are currently youth pastors themselves, and one of our gals is a youth pastor in Alaska.

When Mark and I made the decision to help out with the young people, we had no idea we would be planting seeds of our own. What a privilege it was to reach out and grow with them through some of the most difficult years of their lives. The journey to adulthood isn't easy. As I look back on those years I have come to realize that I needed them more than they needed me. They enriched my life, and taught me the true meaning of unconditional love.

Thrive

Jennifer Knox

Job 8:11-13 Can reeds thrive without water?
While still growing and uncut, they wither
more quickly than grass. Such is the destiny
of all who forget God.

This is a call out to all those diehard gardeners. I looked up the definition of "diehard," and found that it means someone who continues to support something in spite of opposition. So this isn't a call out to the superior gardener, you know, the ones who seem to have no opposition in their garden. This is for the gardener who has nothing but opposition in their flowering oasis. If that's you, then you are my kindred spirit.

My husband and I decided several years ago to turn our boring little yard into Better Homes and Garden. We brought in close to fifty tons of dirt, all of which we shoveled ourselves. Next, we took a bonus check and converted it into trees. Not just one or two trees... more like fifty trees! And not just trees, we bought shrubs, flowers, perennials, annuals, you name it... we got it!

One of the perks of buying from a large retailer of trees and plants, is that you have one year to return anything that did not survive. So, we kept our very large receipt and watched over our new thriving paradise. Hours were spent watering, pruning, fertilizing and praying over each one.

At the one year mark, to our delight, most of our labor had resulted in healthy, growing trees and shrubs. But that was not the fate of all. Many of our evergreens had not held true to their name, and were now looking more like everyellows. So, we gathered up our receipt and loaded up the trees to return, just days before our one year expiration. Now mind you, there were three pallets full of dead trees! It made quite a stir in the garden department. They no longer were excited about their one year offer that they had so boldly boasted about the year before. In fact, they wouldn't honor their agreement and said they would need to keep the trees and have a manager come and look it over.

My fairly humiliated husband left the store only to get a call from them about an hour later. He was told that he could come redeem his money because by some sort of accident, the trees had been thrown away before the manager had arrived! I was thrilled! My husband was horrified, because he had to make the trek back into the store and by now everyone was familiar with "the tree man." Needless to say, our trees had not thrived, but we did get our money back.

By now, I was feeling rather down about our ability to grow things when something strange happened. I walked into our bathroom downstairs and saw something green coming from the drain of the sink. At closer inspection, I realized my sink was sprouting! I left it there to show our company that evening, and by the time they got there to see it, it had grown even more! Now it had leaves on it and was almost three inches long!

Our guests found it repulsive and yet were compelled to keep looking at it. It's not often you can see a plant coming from a sink drain. After doing some asking around, we discovered that my girls had been playing with pumpkin seeds in the sink. One must have gotten loose and, well, the rest is history. I did pull out my little growing pumpkin plant and gave my sink a thorough bleaching to ensure no more plants would pop up.

When I was later talking to a friend of mine about my pumpkin plant, she mentioned how it is like many people. We feel like we are thriving, but really it is just a facade. There is no soil for our roots to take hold of. It is just a matter of time until the storms of life wash us away. My little pumpkin plant was growing, but it could not have thrived and produced fruit in the place it was planted.

How about your life? Are you thriving? Are you planted in the rich soil of God's Word? Are you watered daily with the presence of the Holy Spirit? Do you allow the hard things of life to be the fertilizer that makes you grow strong? Have you placed yourself firmly in the hands of your loving Father? This is how we truly thrive.

The Moving House

Margie McCready

1 Peter 2:5 You also, like living stones, are being built into a spiritual house.

I love to rise early in the morning. There is something about the early morning that intrigues me. I enjoy how quiet it is and how the whole world seems to still be sleeping. I have a morning routine. I love routines. One of the first things I do every morning is look out my front door window. I never know what I am going to see. Some mornings I don't see anything out of the ordinary, but usually that is not the norm. One particular morning I saw a pack of coyotes running right down the middle of the road. Not altogether, but in a straight line, each one about 20 seconds behind the other one. There were five altogether. It made me shudder, as sometimes I walk that early. "Imagine meeting them", I thought. These were not your run of the mill scraggly looking varmints. They were obviously very well fed, to the point where at first glance, I thought they were wolves.

Another morning there was a huge four-point buck right next to my porch eating my English box hedge. He was a magnificent looking creature, and not at all intimidated by my presence. It took some major shooing to get him out of my yard. He exited very slowly looking back at me as if to say, "What's your problem lady?"

One morning I was extremely tired. I drug myself out of bed and headed down to the living room to turn up the heat and catch my usual glance out the front door window. I was stunned by what I saw. Right in front of our home was a huge house slowly moving up the road! It could barely fit on the width of the road. It was a beautiful house, completely finished and made of solid wood. The exterior was a magnificent color with contrasting trim that really made the house "pop". I had to go outside and take a second look. I immediately opened the door and ventured out. For ten minutes I watched this enormous house slowly moving until it went out of sight. I was shocked at how small the trailer was that it was balancing on. "Why doesn't it just slide off", I thought. Our road is anything but smooth. Then I noticed it. The foundation. It was thick and solid. Very solid.

I instantly thought of my own life. The Bible says we are spiritual houses for the Lord to dwell in. He does not dwell in temples built by human hands. He lives in us. It also says to make sure we build our life on the solid foundation which is Jesus Christ. As the familiar song says, "all other ground is sinking sand."

That house made it to its destination. The builder was smart and made sure it had a firm foundation. He knew it was solid. Let us make sure our lives are planted firmly on the solid Rock.

Rustle Up Some Praise

Patty Knox

Psalms 96:12 Let the fields be jubilant, and everything in them; let all the trees of the forest sing for joy.

There is this messy pine tree that copped a squat not far from my front door and just a smidgen east of the front sidewalk that leads to the porch. I give you these location details because this tree's precise location is what sets my teeth on edge and gives me grief. Mr. Fir Tree has not only made himself at home here, but has taken it upon himself daily to tip his hat and empty its contents on my sidewalk. Some days he just pelts down pine needles galore scattering them up and down the walkway that leads to my front porch. It has created a huge mess for me not only outside but inside as well when these little pine needles make their way into my house via foot traffic.

I have had thoughts of taking an axe to the trunk of that tree every time I sweep or rake up its mess. However, Bob, my husband likes the thing. For some odd reason he has bonded with Mr. Hardwood (maybe because he never cleans up after him). Truly here, if I could have a nickel for every pine needle I have swept up after I would be one rich old bird and could hire someone else to deal with the messy things.

A few months back, I stood under Mr. Mess and surveyed the damage from the day before. I stood with broom in hand and stared at the huge clutter before me and suddenly I snapped. With narrowed eyes I slowly began making contact with every single limb on that tree. Then it hit me, the time had come for some serious intervention. If this meant war, then so be it. I was up to the challenge.

I marched in military fashion to the garage to choose my weapon of warfare. Bob had three saws in his arsenal, but I was uncertain as to which weapon would work to my advantage so I followed David's lead when he stood before Saul trying to find what would work best on that giant Goliath. I ended up picking the saw that fit the best in my hand. I gripped my weapon of choice and returned to the battlefield, took my place on the bench and was front and center with the enemy's branches.

I paused for just a brief moment to go over my battle plan. Because of Bob's attachment to the big lug I couldn't attack at the base. However, by hacking off all the lower appendages, I could help disarm the incoming flow of pine needles helping to cut off its supply. So with quick action I sank those saw blade teeth right in the enemy's arm. With fierce jerks and a sudden halt from my saw being stuck I soon realized this branch was not going down without a fight.

So leaning in with all the strength this soldier could muster up, I gave that weapon a pull and a tug and the next thing I knew, the branch snapped and went one way while the saw flew off in another direction and I did a cannonball and shot off that bench and rolled down my yard. If a bush hadn't broken my fall I would probably still be rolling!

I had to retreat into the house due to a twisted ankle. I wasn't about to look up and see the smirks of victory coming from those branches. I had fought a good fight and lost. I surrendered to pine needles. Then Bob came to my rescue and removed all the lower branches and the pine needles dwindled.

While I was convalescing from my wound, the Lord dropped a truth into my heart about that tree out front. He showed me that I was so busy looking down at the mess, that I failed to see the beauty of His creation in the way that Bob did. He was able to see God's handiwork while I only saw work.

I had to confess to the Lord that I have been guilty of this in my Christian life also. I can get so fixated and distracted with the clutter and messes in my life and in others that I fail to see the good things right in front of my own front door. I guess if the trees can rustle up some praise, and sing for joy, like it says in Psalms 96:12 then I can rustle up some praise of my own!

Grandma's Artwork

Patty Knox

Isaiah 49:16 See, I have engraved you on the palms of my hands.

I was busy going from room to room making a last minute check to see that everything was in order for my guests that were soon to arrive. I had just stepped down into my living room when my attention was drawn down to a lower section of wall next to the step. It was scattered with tiny handprints and smudges of various shapes and sizes.

My cleaning instinct nudged me to retreat back to the kitchen to get the spray bottle and give that wall its well needed shower but my Grandma instinct bid me to look closer. These tiny handprints I recognized as those of my three little grandchildren at the time, Ashton, Faith and Brandon. Since then I have added fourteen new sets of handprints to my collection for which I am indeed thankful

As I knelt down to get a closer view, I spotted Ashton's handprints first as they were the biggest and plastered everywhere! At the age of two now, he made many trips up and down the stairs that led in and out of the living room with the help of the wall. This helped to steady his little legs when he stepped down into the room or stepped up out of the room.

The step down for Ashton meant playing with toys from Grandma's toy box or sitting on my lap for a story. The step up for the little tike meant adventures with Grandpa outside, whether it was taking a wheelbarrow ride or looking at the big hammer in Grandpa Bob's toolbox. All of Ashton's handprints had a fun time attached to them, and memories for us.

The smaller handprints and little smudges were those of Brandon and Faith who were both ten months old and playful cousins. This season of life found them cute, cuddly, curious and crawling everywhere! These little culprits autographed the wall every time they planned an escape from the "no no" step out of the room that would lead them to new vistas like Grandma's pantry, or on a good day, a trek all the way to the many steps that led up to Grandpa's study. Yep, no doubt about it, these tiny handprints held adventures for them also.

As I gazed at that wall I suddenly found myself being ushered down memory lane to a season when my four children were making their first marks in this world. And not just the the walls were these handprints found, but the windows, doors, refrigerator, sinks, bathtub and everywhere else they traveled. I even had one son leave his finger creativity marks by coloring all over his bed sheets (think I put that lad to bed too early).

After another step down memory lane I felt my heartstrings stir as if the finger of God himself had nudged them ever so gently. I found myself wishing if only for a day that I could go back and witness my little one's finger prints from a yesterday now gone by.

Ya know? I don't believe I would be so quick on the trigger of the spray bottle this time. I wouldn't rush to erase the evidence of their adventures here and there. I believe I would take some time and identify each handprint and then with a thankful heart for the joy they brought into my life, I would gently kiss each one. Next, I would step back into that day and instead of scolding my young son for the extra work it would cost mommy for erasing those color crayon marks, I would look for the creativity of the lions and tigers and bears he was drawing. And with the few seconds remaining in that day I would graciously give thanks to the good Lord above for the privilege of mothering those four little smudge makers that He placed in my care (Jason, Micah, Nathan and Alison).

Gently dusting off the cobwebs of my memories, I once again returned my attention to the wall. Ashton's handprints suddenly took on a transformation and became a piece of valuable artwork! And the tiny smudges from Brandon and Faith were not smudges at all but little love notes that were telling Grandma how much they enjoyed their visit.

Overcome and teary eyed I came to the conclusion in that moment the spray bottle would just have to stay right where it was, safely tucked under the kitchen sink. After all, before I knew it my grandchildren, like my own children, would someday be bounding in and out of my living room without any further assistance from the wall.

Isn't it strange how a word can suddenly take on a new meaning? As a busy mom, handprints and smudges have only one meaning and that is 'WORK' yet crossing over into grandmother land it transforms into a new meaning which is now 'ARTWORK.'

I'm comforted by the scripture that I chose for this story because it tells me that the Lord has permanently written our names on the palms of His hands. Hence not just one hand, but both as a double reminder that no spray bottle in this world can erase the fact that He loves us dearly. And when He gazes into His palms, He too beholds His children's priceless value and great worth.

The Robe

Margie McCready

Isaiah 61:10 For he has clothed me with garments of salvation and arrayed me in a robe of his righteousness.

The auditorium was packed. People were lined up and overflowing into the halls. It was the spring of 1991 and six very nervous and excited girls were waiting for the judge's decision. One of them would be crowned queen!

The anticipation of the crowd hung like a thick cloud and everyone was on the edge of their seats. My own heart was pounding in my chest. My daughter, Melanie, was one of the finalists and we had spent many months preparing for this one final night. Our town has a festival every year and one fortunate lady gets to wear the title of Queen. She had worked very hard. Much preparation goes into these pageants. Many community functions and writing speeches that require late night hours and loss of precious sleep. Her talent act that night was incredible. She had prepared a lengthy speech that she memorized and had donned a costume becoming our own symbol of freedom, the statue of liberty. We rented the finest costume we could find and I am sure it weighed more then she did. She looked dazzling! She recited her speech perfectly. It was flawless. I held my breath the entire time. When she spoke her very last sentence, she raised the torch to the sky. The gesture was powerful. The crowd erupted in applause and stood on their feet. We all felt one common bond right then – we were proud to be Americans.

It was now time to crown the queen. The two princesses had already been announced and my daughter was not one of them. The once loud stadium was now in a hushed silence. You could have heard a pin drop. I could hear the beating of my own heart. It felt like it took forever, but the judge finally presented us with our queen. When he spoke my daughter's name I jumped out of my seat. I wanted to rush the stage, but knew I would have to wait. I watched through tear filled eyes as they placed the sparkling crown on her head. But what affected me the most was the robe they covered her with. It was beautiful, burgundy crushed velvet and definitely meant for royalty. I instantly saw myself being covered by Jesus with His robe of righteousness. The tears began to fall. Zechariah 3:4 says, "See, I have taken away your sin, and I will put fine garments on you." Think about it! We are royalty! The next time you are feeling insignificant, just remember who you are! Or should I say….Whose you are. You are a child of the King. There could be no greater honor. My daughter Melanie loved being a queen, and I loved being the mother of a queen….at least for one year. That is when her reign ended. Unlike her reign that only lasted a year, we will reign forever!!

If that doesn't get you excited, then nothing will.

Open Mouth Insert Foot

Margie McCready

1 Peter 2:23 When they hurled their insults at him, he did not retaliate; when he suffered, he made no threats.

It was a beautiful Saturday morning. I decided to go out for breakfast with my friend Lisa. We chose a restaurant in town with the best coffee. They also had very good food; organic and tasty. It was one of the smaller places in town, but we didn't care. At least not at first. As we settled into our seats, I looked around like I always do to scope out the surroundings. We were tucked in a corner which was fine with us. Not far from us was a table of four. The restaurant was not busy. I was surprised. *This will be enjoyable,* I thought. My enjoyment ended quickly when I began to overhear the man at the table talking. I heard the word "Christian" and my senses and ears perked up like a hound dog's. I recognized instantly from his words that he was "bashing Christians." I was appalled! How dare he! *We are the nicest people on the planet,* I thought (pride goes before a fall). My face was turning red and my heart was pounding in my chest. Lisa told me to ignore him. "Who cares," she said, "he is lost." I tried to ignore him but the more he spoke, the angrier I became.

I finally did what I should have done in the beginning; I prayed. "God help me." Deep down I wanted to knock him out of his chair. I felt so much better after I prayed and thought I had a handle on things until these words came out of his mouth: "The reason our world is so messed up is because of all the Christians. They are nothing but cancers in society." I lost it. I thought I was going to explode! I was so outraged at this point that all my good prayers flew right out the window. I got out of my chair and did what any Christian would do who was reacting in the flesh; I blasted him with both barrels. It wasn't pretty. He was absolutely furious. I had embarrassed him in front of his friends. I saw the fury and hatred in his eyes and quickly headed for the exit so he couldn't respond to what I had just said to him. He was beyond mad. He followed me out to my car yelling profanities and cursing me. I honestly thought he was going to hit me. I jumped in my car and sped off before he could block me from leaving. Lisa sat in the car with a stone face. As I pulled out, I could see him in my rearview mirror shaking his fist at me. "I showed him," I said. She just looked at me and said, "Was it worth it?" The words haunted me all the way home.

It wasn't long before the Holy Spirit began to deal with me. I felt justified; what was I supposed to do? He deserved it. I asked myself "What would Jesus have done?" The answer took the wind right out of my sails; "Buy his breakfast." Ouch. I blew it. I was 100% in the wrong.

You and I will face a lot of injustice in this world. Jesus, himself, told us we would. How do we handle it correctly? The same way He did. It is called restraint. He will give us the power to do it. No matter how tempting it is, we are not to return evil for evil. My response was carnal. It is not up to us to right every wrong and defend God. He can take care of Himself. Our goal is to be Christ-like in all of our actions and especially in what comes out of our mouths. He quietly endured. For the sake of the gospel and our own Christian testimony we must do the same. I remembered the scripture that said when Jesus was being insulted and persecuted that he kept silent and did not open His mouth. Jesus chose to let His life speak for itself. I burst into tears and repented.

We live in a small town. I told the Lord if I ever saw him again I would apologize. Fortunately for me, he must have been a tourist.

Amazing grace.

New Beginnings

Patty Knox

Revelation 21:5 He who was seated on the throne said, "I am making everything new!"

I have always felt bad for folks who have lost homes due to a fire or natural disasters like hurricanes, tornados and earthquakes. What it must feel like to see your place of safety and security reduced to ashes or a heap of rubble. Our homes, besides our families, are extremely important to us because they offer us a sanctuary of rest and personal familiarity. Our home is where we share our personal lives with family and store memories long after the last child has left the nest.

Homes certainly hold a lot of drama, problems and challenges of all kinds too, but at the end of the day when everyone is bedded down for the night, this abode still offers a safe dwelling and a hope that things will work out because you are bonded together by a knowledge that no matter what, families stick together.

I love to think about all the celebrations that take place in our houses. Birthday parties, holidays, bridal and baby showers, plus graduations, just to name a few. Family and friends gathered together to enjoy each other's company in a safe and warm environment.

All of this is fresh in my thoughts today because I recently experienced seeing my childhood home with all its surrounding buildings completely demolished! Leveled entirely to the ground. Not even one stick of wood or a small piece of crumbled foundation laid in its aftermath. It was as if life as I had known it had vanished right before my eyes.

Oh, I knew this would be happening when we sold our folk's land to the Salmon Coalition Foundation. The plan was to turn the land once again into its natural habitat. But seeing fifty-eight years of memories swept away was an experience that caused me to catch my breath.

Then I was reminded of the passage of scripture in the book of Revelation, chapter twenty-one where the bible speaks of a new dwelling that will be coming out of Heaven from God. Where He will wipe away every tear from our eyes and there will be no more death or sorrow, crying or pain, for all the old things will pass away and He will make everything new.

This comforts me immensely as I may no longer see my mother hanging towels on the clothesline or standing at the door ready to greet me with a smile in this life, but I know by faith that I will see her once again when all things become new.

My dad no longer can be seen chopping wood, feeding his cows or standing amidst a pack of dogs with wagging tails, yet when all the former things of this life are gone I shall see him once more.

My oldest sister Karen had physical limitations in this life and was never able to run but limped around our driveway while the rest of us eight siblings ran. But the Lord assures me that in making all things new, that death and pain will be erased and I will see Karen run in His new kingdom.

Revelation 21:5 states, He who was seated on the throne said, "I am making everything new" then he said, "write this down, for these words are trustworthy and true." When we face loss or barren places in this life. When negative circumstances have leveled our faith, hope and trust, causing us to see only desolate wasteland. Let us take hold of the blueprints of the heavenly house that God is preparing for all of us. Let us study the rooms that will bring us face to face with Him and our loved ones. A house where death, sorrow, tears and pain will not enter. Let's take hold of the truth that someday all things will become "new."

There's Meaning in a Name

Jennifer Knox

John 12:14-15 Jesus found a young donkey and sat upon it, as it is written, "Do not be afraid... see, your king is coming, seated on a donkey's colt."

Names fascinate me. I loved naming my children, and would name other people's children if they'd let me. My husband (whose name is Micah, a name I have LOVED since I was 11... and also a good Bible name!) and I had already picked our first child's name long before we ever had her. Back when I was still in college we would sit around and think of names we would like to name our children. We both loved the name Faith, and to my delight, several years later we would be holding our little Faithy. Next we had a little girl named Hope. So when we found out that our third child was going to be a girl we were in a bit of a quandary. Here we had a Faith and a Hope and it seemed a little strange to jump from the unintended theme and go with a name I had always loved... Faith, Hope and Janelle. Nope, we were going with the theme now. Then the question was, do we name her Grace or Joy? My husband made the final call on that one, and we now have our sweet Grace! When we were informed that our forth child was a boy, we were already set to name him Justice. I love the name Justice. It's strong, plus it says in Isaiah, "For I, the LORD, love justice." I'll never forget the day when my daughter Faith was about six years old. She came home from church and commented on her and her sibling's names, "Mommy, did you know our names are things?" I am thrilled that to this day, each of my kids love their names!

A friend once mentioned what it must be like at the Knox household hearing, "Faith! Hope! Grace! Justice!" shouted out all day. I proceeded to inform our friend that it was more than that. We have two dogs as well. Since we believe there is no need to stop a good thing, and our name picking ability was definitely a good thing, we chose to follow suit with our canine family. We have a female named Mercy (actually she is the THIRD Mercy dog we've had, but that's a topic for another day). I like to call her Princess, because she believes she is true royalty and should be treated as such. That brings me to our male dog. I will say this, he was named by my husband… his name is Judgement. Now Judgement is not a fitting name for such a puffalumpy (that is his rightful name!). He is unaware that his name is Judgment, and answers to the name Puffy, Puffy Face or Puffalumpers, all much more fitting names for such a squishy face (another name he answers to).

Then there are nick-names. A nick-name is a peek into a person's life. As teenagers many of us disdain our given pseudo-names, only to cherish them later in life. I had given my cousin Heidi the name "Heidrack" when we were in elementary school. Heidi's name gave our grandmother much angst, seeing how their family dog was named Heidi. She never felt it an appropriate name for a human, let alone her beloved granddaughter! A year after I had started calling my cousin "Heidrack," she came home and informed me that she had learned where I had come up with the name! She read the book I read in which Heidrack was the name of the dog! "I've been named after a dog twice!" she informed me with disgust. However, my term of endearment stuck even after all these years. Speaking of dogs, allow me to digress for just a moment. My little niece, Sabrina, had a dog named Scarpa. I just loved the way she would say her name, Sabima, so I would continually prompt her to repeat it by asking, "Is your name Scarpa?" To which she'd respond, "No, I'm Sabima!" It just didn't get old hearing her say, "I'm Sabima!" So over and over I'd ask her. Finally, after about the hundredth time I asked, "Is your name Scarpa?" My little five year old niece replied, "Yup!" I think she gave up hope on ever teaching her aunt what her real name was!

So, what's all this fuss about names? I'm glad you asked! That leads me to my name, Jennifer. There's nothing out-and-out wrong with my name. It was a very... let me say that again... a VERY popular name in the year I was born! Apparently there was not a lot of communication among parents that year, and no one seemed to notice that ALL their pregnant friends were choosing the name Jennifer for their dear little girls! In my class of thirty kids, seven, yes SEVEN of us were named Jennifer! On my soccer team there were so many Jennifers that we had to go by initials like: JW, JR, JC etc. The only problem was that there were Jennifers with the same initials! So, by the time I was getting my new given name for the soccer year, my initials were already claimed. I was stuck with reversing my initials and was called BJ for the rest of the year.

Before you feel too bad for me, which I would appreciate some sympathy in the matter, I didn't actually go by Jennifer during those years. I went by Jenny. That's the name many of my family members still call me. I felt it was important to find out the meaning of my name since a name is part of one's identity! The Bible mentions several times how a person's name speaks to their destiny and identity. As I was looking up the meaning of my name, I was filled with anticipation at what I would find. Maybe Jenny meant graceful, beautiful, delicate, or jewel of great value! Or possibly it was something strong like warrior, valiant, fearless! It was almost too much to bear knowing I was about to find out my true identity! To my complete dismay, I stared as I saw the word before me. It was just one word, not a list of words as I had often seen attached to the meaning of a name. Nope... just one! The word I read... "Donkey!" Yes! Donkey! Had my parents not considered the fact that there is meaning and destiny in a name? Had they overlooked that there's power in a name? Not only did I have the most unoriginal name in the universe, my identity was forever... Donkey! It was a crushing blow.

As I pondered the fact that I was donkey woman, I wondered what that said about me. I tried to find the good in it, but we all know that being called Donkey (or worse, its OTHER name) is anything but good! That is until the Lord showed me something so sweet. What could be sweet about being called Donkey your entire life? Well, leave it up to the Lord to take our tragedy and turn it into triumph. What was it that carried Jesus into His triumphal entry into Jerusalem? You got it… a donkey! Yes, the lowly donkey got to usher the King of Kings into the great city of Jerusalem. Even lowly donkey me, can have the privilege of ushering the Kingdom of God into a desperately needy world. I can share the amazing love of Jesus with those who are hurting, broken and crushed in spirit. A mere donkey was given the amazing honor of being close to Jesus on that great day! And now, not only this donkey (being me), but each of us have that same honor. The King doesn't ride on our backs, but actually lives within us! He wants to live THROUGH us to reach a world that He desperately loves! So see, there IS meaning in a name! To some, Donkey might seem a curse to be called, but to me… I see it as a chance to usher in The King!

Newy Dogs

Jennifer Knox

Romans 2:4 Or do you show contempt for the riches of his kindness, forbearance and patience, not realizing that God's kindness is intended to lead you to repentance?

Ever heard of a Newy Dog? At first glance one might think it's a hot dog you'd buy from a street vendor as you strolled some New England road. That'd make sense... Newy Dog. Or maybe it conjures up some new slang for greeting one's friend... similar to "wassup dog?!" It adds a new dimension to the phrase by asking the question of what's new with your "dog" friend... "What's Newy Dog?"... (aka: what's new friend?). Well, if this is where your mind goes, you're not alone. I had no idea what a Newy Dog was either, until I married into the Newy Dog family!

My husband, Micah, and I were born in the same year, on the same coast of the United States, in the same financial status. Neither of our families had much money, but we both had great childhoods. Having some things in common did not mean we had all things in common. I grew up with very wealthy grandparents. My grandfather was a surgeon and also a savvy investor. I spent my summers in Southern California enjoying fine dining, fancy restaurants, high-end shopping, lounging around at the beach or on my grandparent's patio overlooking the ocean.

My husband loved, and I mean LOVED going to his grandparent's house. It was over in Quilcene, Washington, a very small logging town where his mom grew up. His grandma was affectionately called Grandma Newy (named after their last name of Newman). Everything I've ever heard about her is amazing. She did not have much in way of earthly possessions, but what she lacked in things, she made up for with love. She had nine children, which produce a boatload of grandchildren. She had a drawer stocked full of candies for her grandchildren to eagerly search through. She made wonderful meals and had a sense of humor to beat all. They owned a large plot of land, and my husband would spend his days hunting for ducks, bucking brush, fishing in the river or swimming in the bay.

The first time I went out to the Newy property I was amazed that so many children could grow up in such a tiny home! This house might have been tiny, but my first real impression was, "Boy, it's hot in here!" There was a wood stove in the corner that pumped out the heat like nothing I've ever felt! I was certain that these kids never suffered from cold! My mother-in-law walked me all around, sharing memories of her and her siblings. I would try and picture her playing dolls, roller skating or riding bikes right there where we were standing. That's when I was jolted from memory lane and about knocked off my feet! It was a Newy Dog! Now, to explain a Newy Dog, I must back up a moment. As sweet and gentle as Grandma Newy was, Grandpa Newy was exactly the opposite. He was a gruff man with a hot temper. I was always sad when I would think of all the hurtful things he had done or said to my mother-in-law (whom, I will add, is one of the sweetest people you'd ever meet... she must have taken after her mom!). His choice means of communication was to yell, and yell he did! Now, for all the rough edges he had, he also had a tender side, which he mostly chose to share with his dogs.

Now, one would think that if one wanted to show affection to one's dogs, that one would speak kindly, gently, affectionately... well, that wasn't the Newy way! Grandpa Newy showed his love by boiling them chickens, giving them their own house to live in. No... really... the dogs had their own house! Grandpa Newy owned the old house next to his, and decided this would make a fitting house for his beloved dogs. He made sure they were comfortable by adding a radio to keep them serenaded to sleep each night. These dogs were HUGE, and not necessarily because of their breed. Nope, they were as my mother-in-law put it, walking pigs! They grunted and snorted as they walked with their fat bellies, but they were happy, fat, pig dogs! Grandpa Newy spoiled them, but always spoke with that infamous booming voice! "GET BACK! GET BACK!" he'd yell, then dole out the chicken he'd boiled just for them. Now I'm not even sure dogs are supposed to eat chickens, but these dogs did, and they loved it... they loved him!

One night several years ago, my husband and I took a drive over to Quilcene. It was late by the time we arrived and no one was home. As my husband, Micah, got out of the truck, he was met by the Newy Dogs, and let me say, they were not too happy to see him! What I saw next I never would've believed if I hadn't seen it with my own eyes! My husband started trying to win the dogs over by sweetly saying, "Hi puppy, it's ok!" You know, the way most people talk to a dog when you greet them. The more he spoke to them the more they growled. I thought, "Oh man! He's going down!" Then my husband changed his approach. Being a Newy himself, he started to mimic his grandpa's harsh voice, "GET BACK! GET BACK!" With that, those big, fat, pig dogs started wagging their tails, tongues hanging out, bellies flopping side to side. They were actually happier the more he yelled at them! Once he thought he had them won over, he switched back to "normal people talk." Immediately the dogs were on guard and started to growl. Now they may be fat, pig dogs, but you don't want to mess with an aggressive, fat, pig dog! So back he went to yelling at them… and back they went to being happy. He was able to walk right over to them, tails a waggin', as long as he kept yelling. It was one of the oddest things I'd ever seen!

Well, many years have passed since then, but I was reminded of the story as I sat watching a church conference online. Several of the pastors were making sarcastic digs at the congregation and they all would laugh. At one point the audience stood up to welcome a pastor and he said, "SHUT UP! SIT DOWN! I don't have time for that!" The congregation laughed heartily as they sat down, and I thought back to the Newy Dogs. We have been so pumped full of hate, rejection and criticism, that many of us respond affectionately towards that.

In some twisted way many have become comfortable with being recipients of sarcasm and hurtful words. There are those who no longer know how to accept a compliment or know how to respond to a kind word spoken to them, even in the church. This is completely contrary to our Heavenly Father. Our God is a God of love and kindness. It says in Romans 2:4, "Or do you show contempt for the riches of his kindness, forbearance and patience, not realizing that God's kindness is intended to lead you to repentance?" I wonder how many of us do not know how to respond to a loving God. Many of us are only comfortable with an angry God who wants to drop the hammer on us at any moment, but that's not His character. He loves us. Hosea 2:14 tells how God will speak tenderly to us, even to those who have rejected Him. I pray that today, tomorrow and for the rest of our days, we will hear the voice of our loving Heavenly Father as He draws us with His kind and gentle words.

The Gift of Life

Margie McCready

Psalm 119:73 Your hand made me and formed me.

It was a late evening in June. I was standing in the operating room dressed in blue garb, feeling very much like a fish out of water. I was staring at my grandson who had just been delivered by cesarean section six weeks earlier than his scheduled due date. As the surgeon held him up, I felt like someone had knocked the wind out of me. I thought I was going to faint. He was far too small, and my first and only thought was "put him back, he is not done". All of my babies were close to 9 pounds (except the twins, of course). They were roly poly, chubby babies with beautiful color. This baby was only 3 pounds and had grayish skin that appeared to be stretched over his bones. All his veins were visible right through him as though he were transparent.

What happened next startled me back to reality. He let out a huge piercing scream, followed by loud outbursts of crying. His lungs were completely developed! Color began to slowly cascade over his skin. I was expecting them to whisk him away and hook him up to oxygen, but this little guy was maintaining very well on his own, thank you! It was a miracle. I burst into tears.

Earlier that day my daughter phoned me from the doctor's office. It was supposed to be just a routine prenatal visit. It was anything but routine. "Mom," she said, "there is something wrong; the baby needs to come out today." My tongue stuck in my throat and my heart started pounding in my chest. I finally said, "I'll be right there." Fortunately for me, the clinic was only a mile away. As I walked into the doctor's office my only thought was, "These newfangled doctors drive me crazy. They are always looking for a reason to bring these babies into the world before their time. They probe too much, pick and poke too much rather than just leaving them alone." My daughter was only 17 and visibly upset. I asked her to wait outside so I could talk to the doctor alone. When her doctor saw the look on my face, she immediately started talking. "Margie, this baby needs to be delivered. Now. It is not getting the proper nutrition it needs." I was shaking and trying to compose myself. I looked at her and said, "The only way this baby is being born today is if you can prove to me his life is in danger." She then showed me the ultrasound picture. "We don't know what causes this," she said, "but for some reason the placenta has been signaled that the baby has been delivered. It is drying up and no longer sending the proper nourishment to the baby." I looked closely at the cord in the picture and indeed the line was very thin. I was holding back the tears. "Your grandson will slowly starve to death," she said. He was not due for 6 weeks. I felt numb.

Back in the operating room I was comforting my daughter as best I could. They showed her the baby and then quickly exited the room. He was still crying; a very good sign. The surgeon motioned me to the other side of the curtain. "I want to show you the placenta," she said. I looked down and I was amazed at what I saw. Sure enough, it was drying from the inside out. There was only a very small portion that was still alive and functioning. Her decision that day saved my grandson's life. When I could finally speak, I apologized to the doctor for being so angry and feeling that she was overreacting. She was very gracious.

My grandson was perfect! The doctors were even amazed. At only 3 pounds he was completely developed, even his tiny little lungs. They told us before he was born that he would most likely remain in the hospital for at least 30 days. They were anticipating all the complications that can arise with a premature baby. There were none. Not one. It was as if he was delivered full term (except for his weight). Even our cat weighed more than he did! My daughter brought him home in 10 days. She named him Solomon. What a delight he was! I wouldn't let him cry, because I didn't want him to exert any more energy than he needed to. I wanted him to use all his energy to grow and put on weight. I hardly ever put him down. What a gift from the Lord he was!

He is 11 years old now and excels at everything he puts his mind to. He is also a granny's boy...(but don't tell anyone, I wouldn't want to embarrass him)!

Two Peas in a Pod

Patty Knox

Ruth 1:16 Where you go I will go, and where you stay I will stay. Your people will be my people and your God my God.

Yep! Two peas in a pod, that's Jennifer and I. Let me give you a little background history on the two of us that has kept us snuggled together like two peas in a pod for many years. First off, besides sharing the same last name due to the fact that she is married to my son Micah, she is also the mother of four of my treasured grandchildren. Not only that but we are kindred spirit friends.

But that is just the tip of the iceberg on things we have in common. Another thing is our hair. You know the type of hair that is soft and manageable? Well, that is not our hair. We both have come to the conclusion that we don't have normal hair follicles but mutated ones that left us with hair like a bale of straw that is hard to contend with. Once we had a contest to see whose hair bale held more straw by ratting it with a comb. Jennifer swears to this day that she won. The truth is If we both walked into a room together with exploded hair follicles you would have to open the windows to let some of the pressure out of the frizz.

I am sure we share carpal tunnel syndrome too from trying to tame our wild straw beasts with our hairbrushes. Thankfully now we both have found a weapon that helps keep the mane under control with the use of our flatirons.

Here is something else we have in common, we like to go on walks. Now, Jennifer disagrees that we are alike when we take walks together. She says she likes to keep her eyes straight ahead on course and keep the pace while she implies that I, on the other hand (or should I say foot), likes to take in all the scenery around me and divert off the intended path. She came to this conclusion one day when we were out walking and I noticed an empty house in our neighborhood with a for sale sign out front. I acknowledge I led us on a small detour to check out the place and peek inside the windows.

Now, I will also admit that Jennifer is never keen to these unexpected turns or off ramp exits that I take us on. She says this makes her nervous. She reminds me of previous walks together and of stumbling over broken planters and scratchy shrubs just to make our way to a window to get a gander of empty rooms! This annoyance is followed up with caution and concern that people could still be residing in the house itself. *Relax dear, that's why you have me in your pod.*

Well, it took some persuading but Jennifer finally agreed to my coaxing but warned me this was the very last time she was getting off the beaten path when we walked together. Assuring her that the house was empty we climbed a ton of steps to the front door and then plowed through some bushes to get to the big plate glass window. Plastering our faces to the glass with our hands cupped around our heads, we leaned our bodies in to get a good look. The living room indeed was empty but as we looked toward the dining room, a table and chairs were intact and a woman was walking toward a chair.

Jennifer fell back horrified, threw up her arms and hightailed it out of that yard. I was trailing close behind but instead of being distraught I can't remember when I had had such an amusing walk. I burned more calories that day from laughing than I did from walking! I think the reverse was true for my pea pal. Needless to say, from that time on I have been on my own for those adventures. But I'm still claiming we are two peas in a pod.

Jennifer and I also have common ministries when it comes to teaching at women's conferences and working together in the Sunday School department. Plus, we have similar talents when it comes to dressing up like old babes and making a chic calendar. We have twin nun outfits and have used them in skits. Through the fun times and the sad, the good days and the bad, we have chosen to stay like two peas in a pod.

I have often thought what Naomi would have missed if Ruth had chosen to go back to her land and not journey with Naomi to hers. If you are not familiar with the story of this mother and daughter-in-law, I suggest you read it in the Bible. It is called the book of Ruth and it is a beautiful story of love, devotion and commitment. You might say Naomi and Ruth were two peas in a pod too!

Jennifer, I'm thankful to the Lord for having someone like you to share impossible hair days and to join me in window peeking walks. We have experienced some dark valleys and some mountain top vistas together. We have shared a million laughs and shed some tears. You have enriched my life in so many areas. I have often thought what I would have missed had you not journeyed into our lives. But unlike Naomi's offer to send Ruth in another direction, I'm not sending you anywhere! Because after all, we are two peas in a pod!

The Great Teacher

Margie McCready

1 Timothy 4:13 Until I come, devote yourself to the public reading of Scripture, to preaching and to teaching.

Most of us could look back over our school years and single out that one teacher who made the most impact in our lives. For me, it was a grade school teacher named Miss Fahrety. She was an older spinster with flaming, red-orange hair that stuck out in every direction. She reminded me of a cartoon character. I loved her. How could you not love a teacher who looked like Raggedy Ann? If Raggedy Ann had a mother, I was sure it was Miss Fahrety. My first doll was a Raggedy Ann doll. My mother saved her for me and gave her to me a few years before she died. She had kept her in an old shoe box in her closet. One look at this doll and you can see where she got the name "Raggedy." To me, she is a treasure and very beautiful.

I was fascinated with Miss Fahrety. My favorite time of the day was story time. We would all sit around her on the floor and she would begin to captivate us with the special books she would read out loud to us. She had a way of making books come alive. I wanted to jump right in and become a part of the story. I remember closing my eyes sometimes and pretending I was part of the story. So began my passion for books. She planted the seed in me and then carefully nourished it. "Learn to read, and you can conquer the world," she would say. I believed her.

I remember one particular summer in 1961. She would come to the library every Wednesday and let me check out books to read during summer vacation. Normally you could only check out three at a time, but during the summer there was no limit. I was in heaven! I usually checked out more than I could carry and she would give me a ride home. I devoured those books like fleas on a dog. It was one of the most memorable summers of my life. My favorite book was "Pippi Longstocking." I checked out that book continually and read it over and over again. I dreamed of being Pippi for just one day. She was my hero.

Great teachers not only inspire, they teach by example. Every free minute she had, Miss Faherty had her nose in a book. I thought she was amazing.

I wanted to be just like her. The summer passed too quickly and I was moved up to a new grade and out of her class. I missed her so much. Sometimes I would pass her in the halls and she would always say the same thing to me, "Still reading?" Truth is, I never stopped. Because of her love for books, I am the ultimate book worm today, and very proud of it. She taught me well.

Pippi Longstocking is no longer my favorite book. I met the greatest author of all time in 1970 and His book is now my favorite. I also have a new Hero; His name is Jesus Christ. I am in the Lord's classroom now. Every day I am learning how to better walk with Him. I am trying to be the best student I can possibly be. I want to know everything there is to know about the greatest teacher who ever lived – now I want to be just like Him.

My Cup Runneth Over

Jennifer Knox

Psalm 23:5-6 You prepare a table before me in the presence of my enemies. You anoint my head with oil; my cup overflows. Surely goodness and love will follow me all the days of my life, and I will dwell in the house of the Lord forever.

It was one of those perfect summer mornings in Seattle, they don't happen often, but when they do it's amazing! I woke up and the sun was shining with a beautiful, blue sky. I headed straight outside and set my sprinkler to prepare my grass for the warm day ahead. Then I proceeded to get my coffee and sat myself on the deck to take in the morning.

The birds were singing, the sun was warm, and the gentle motion of the sprinkler created a peaceful scene. I watched as it went back and forth, softly and quietly watering the yard. I was particularly interested in a bird that had made its home under our eaves. It was busy taking care of the baby chicks that had recently been born. I was amazed at how hard this bird worked. Off she would go to get food and quickly return with something in her mouth. She would only be in the nest a moment before she was off again to hunt for more.

As I was enjoying the sights and sounds and sipping my coffee, in came mama bird again. She was coming in for her descent over my head when all of a sudden something fell from the heavens and landed smack dab into my coffee cup causing it to overflow! What could that have been? Thank goodness I had chosen a clear glass mug for today's coffee experience. (That is what coffee in the morning is for me... an experience that starts with picking out the perfect mug for the day.)

As I searched for the mysterious object, I lifted up my glass to get a look from the bottom of the mug. That's when I saw it! That bird had pooped in my coffee cup! Little miss busy bird had apparently been too rushed to notice me... on my deck... of my house... that she was squatting on! I immediately felt an eviction notice was comin' on!

How could she have been so rude? Here I was enjoying a perfect summer morning, warmth from the sun, sprinkler going, birds singing, coffee brewed to perfection... then this! Then I started thinking what would have happened had I not noticed what she had done! What if it hadn't splashed and gotten my attention? Immediately I started considering having a phobia of consuming beverages outside. One could never be sure of what could land in a cup without the protection of a ceiling.

I tossed my cup of coffee, and the mug as well. How could I ever drink from that mug knowing what had happened? Nope... its days with me were over. My perfect morning spoiled, my coffee ruined, my mug gone, all because of a rude bird!

Got me thinking, isn't that just like life though? We are going about our life then the "stuff" (sounds so much more ladylike than other words) of life comes our way. We can either choose to toss out the coffee and the cup... or just allow the Lord to wash it clean and fill it back up with His Holy Spirit. We will all have "stuff" fall on us that we didn't expect, but we can always rest in the knowledge that the Lord saw it coming and was already preparing to help us through it. He is just that good. I pray your cup does overflow with joy, laughter and love... but on those days when "stuff" falls into your cup... may you know that the Lord is there to help get you a fresh cup!

Granny I Picked a Giant Pickle in Your Yard

Patty Knox

Ephesians 3:17-18 And I pray that you, being rooted and established in love, may have power, together with all the Lord's holy people, to grasp how wide and long and high and deep is the love of Christ,

I decided last Spring to try my luck with some different fruits and vegetables besides the usual ones that graced my garden. I always enjoy planting tomatoes and cucumbers and even string beans are tasty when picked fresh. I had a spot that could house another plant so I chose a zucchini, being assured it would grow fast and produce so much that I would have an endless supply of the stuff.

So I plopped that little seedling into the ground and waited and waited and waited. However, my little zucchini plant stayed the same size for weeks. It was well into July before that little bugger had a growth spurt. It became established and put on new leaves every day but I failed to see any babies attaching themselves to the vine.

But the rest of my plants were going gangbusters and by the first part of August I had tons of cucumbers in a large pot that were cascading down the sides in all different sizes.

Two of my granddaughters, Faith (five) and Ava (four) who belong to my daughter Alison, love to come visit in the summer and enjoy playing in the backyard. The girls loved pushing their baby dolls in their strollers through the yard but when Ava spied the cucumbers she started plucking them from the vines, wrapping them in napkins and then tossing them in her stroller along with her dolly. Then she got finger yank happy and her cucumber babies multiplied, so much so that we had to start eating them every day.

Curious about my zucchini plant one day, I lifted up a leaf and sure enough we had a baby on the way! It was about six inches long. I was elated until I remembered Ava's obsession with having a large cucumber family. What if she decided she needed one more for her brood and found my little zucchini!

I quickly devised a barrier to keep her away and it worked. She stayed clear and my zucchini kept growing. In the meantime, Ava continued to pick cucumbers and after giving them a ride in her stroller she and I would peel and share them. One particular day while sharing one with Faith and Ava, I explained that some cucumbers were chosen to be pickles. This news absolutely fascinated Ava and I could almost see the wheels rolling in her head.

By the middle of August my zucchini (without any siblings) was well on his way to adulthood. I couldn't wait until September rolled around so I could make bread, muffins, and whatever else I could find recipes for. I was enjoying these thoughts one afternoon when Alison and her girls dropped by for a visit.

I was preparing dinner, and while Alison offered to help, the girlies went outside to play. Before long, Ava trotted in declaring that she has spotted a giant pickle in the yard. Since we had recently had this "pickle" conversation, I was assuming she had spotted a big cucumber. Being humored by this, I replied, "Oh really? Well, why don't you just bring that giant pickle to Granny so I can see it?" She pondered my question for a moment and then informed me that it was too big to bring in. Chuckling to myself I decided to join her in her imaginary giant pickle story and bid her one more time to use her muscles and carry that giant pickle into the house. "Okay Granny, I'll try my best." Then back outside she trotted while her mommy and I had a good laugh over her large pickle story.

After several minutes had passed Ava returned, wiggled her way through the back door and was holding her prize pickle, with leaves, roots and dirt attached to it! She was covered in dust from head to toe and sporting a grin the length of the Mississippi River! "Look Gran, I picked a giant pickle in your yard." With raised eyebrows and dilated eyes I quickly realized this was not Ava's imagination when I witnessed dirt clods dropping to the kitchen floor. I chuckle even now thinking how hard she must have tugged and jerked on my prize zucchini to pull it, roots and all, out of the ground!

My initial disappointment gave way to laughter as I realized I would reap far more in memories from this giant pickle than my zucchini would have yielded in bread or muffins.

The Bible reminds us to be rooted and grounded in love so that we will be able to grasp how wide, high and deep the love of Christ is for us. This assures us all when troubles come our way, that no amount of tugging or pulling can uproot our faith when we are grounded in love.

Christmas

Jennifer Knox

Matthew 7:11 If you, then, though you are evil, know how to give good gifts to your children, how much more will your Father in heaven give good gifts to those who ask him!

I love Christmas! I love the decorations, I love the baking, I love the smells, I love the lights, I love the stockings all hung in a row, really I love just about everything involving Christmas. My parents made Christmas a wonderful time for me and my sister growing up. We had our family tradition of Christmas light looking on Christmas Eve, then my sister and I would sleep in the living room and try to fall asleep. I say try, because Christmas Eve was always the hardest night to sleep. I was giddy with delight that my sister was spending the night with me (that's what we called it when she'd let me sleep with her as she was four years older than me) and at the fact that a stocking would soon be laid by my head.

Of all the highlights of Christmas, stockings are my favorite part. My mom (aka Santa) stuffed a stocking like no other! Our tradition was that my mom would sneak in, once we were finally asleep, and put our stockings by our heads. I usually woke up to the sound of paper crinkling by my pillow, but would never open my eyes until my mom was safely out of sight. As my eyes adjusted to the dim light of the Christmas tree, I would stare at the stocking next to me. I wouldn't dare touch it! That was for morning, but nights were for looking! All the gifts stuffed inside gave our stockings a bulging, contorted look. "Oh! What could be making that sharp poke on the side, and what was that twisty thing shoved out the top?" I'd wonder. There was no telling what they were, because each gift was carefully wrapped and tucked inside the stocking. Not only were our stockings stuffed to capacity, but they were stuffed to overflowing! There would be gifts laid next to our stockings as well!

My parents had a strict rule, no opening stockings until 6:00 am! This potentially meant hours of waiting on our part. My sister and I would watch the clock and at exactly six, we went bounding down our little hallway into my parents' room. "Merry Christmas!"

we'd announce with delight (and no doubt way too loud for sleeping ears)! My parents would smile and drag their tired bodies out of bed and into our living room. Then we could tear into our stockings to find out what had been making those bulges and pokes! Stockings were a free for all, we both opened our stockings at the same time. This was unlike presents, we opened those one at a time to make it last longer, plus we got to see what everyone got.

It's funny how those stockings delighted me. Inside was filled with little things like pencils, toothbrushes, erasers, hair barrettes, nothing expensive, just lots of little things wrapped with lots of love. My parents did not have a lot of money when I was growing up, so I always knew this was a big sacrifice for them, and boy did I love it!

As we moved to the presents, my mom always had us stop and read out of the Bible about the true gift of Christmas, Jesus. We would pray and thank Him for coming and saving us. I loved taking the time to talk to Jesus. Once we even baked Him a birthday cake! Then, slowly we would each take a turn opening up a gift. One person was always designated as "Santa." This person was chosen by a game we played earlier in the Christmas season. The first person to spot Christmas lights that year won twenty-five cents and the title of "Santa." Their duty was to distribute each of the gifts from under the tree. One year I won the coveted "first Christmas light seer" and prepared for my role accordingly! I stuffed my red pajamas with pillows and made my role as Santa official with a hearty "ho ho ho!" as I passed out each gift.

Well, not much has changed over the years, only now I am the one who gets to stuff the stockings. And oh, do I love it! I love the process. Over the month I pick up little things like pencils, toothbrushes, erasers, hair barrettes (sound familiar?), then I take a day to wrap. I go into my room and lock the door, and then put on the same Little House on the Prairie, it's the one when Laura buys Ma a stove, but Pa had bought the same one too. I wait and only watch this one at Christmas, then I loop it for the entire time I'm wrapping. Once the stocking stuffers are wrapped, I move on to the gifts. With each one, my heart starts racing at the thought of my children's faces opening their surprise from under the tree. Many Christmases we did not have much money to spend, but even a little gift was such a delight to watch them open!

My four children have carried on my sister and my tradition of sleeping in the living room. Each Christmas Eve they pull out sleeping bags and pillows and nestle down for the LONG night ahead… only theirs isn't as long as mine was (having to wait until 6:00 in the morning!). I go to bed and wait until I think they are asleep (which they usually fake that they are when I go down... just like I used to do) and I start to lay their stockings by their head. The wrapping paper crinkles as I set it by their pillows, but they keep their eyes shut tight, until I walk away. Just like when I was little, the stockings bulge and extra gifts are laid beside each stocking, each little gift wrapped and hidden, leaving little ones to wonder what's inside!

That's when my story as a little girl, and my children's story no longer match. My children actually fall back asleep once they see their stockings, even though they pretend they didn't see them! I'm the mom, I'm supposed to drag my weary body back to bed and fall fast asleep until my little angels come bounding in and wake me up! But NO! I'm too excited! I can't sleep! I just lay there awake, thinking about the stockings laying by my children's heads, thinking about the gifts they will open in the morning... the one they've wanted but don't know they are getting! It's all too much for a love-sick mom! So, around five o'clock in the morning I head back downstairs to where my little ones are sleeping. Then I start to make little noises to try and wake them up. One time I went down at four in the morning to wake them... but no one would stir… not even a mouse! So, I reverted back to five. As their little eyes start to open, I am quick to pounce, for fear they'll roll over and go back to sleep! "Merry Christmas!" I announce with delight (and no doubt STILL too loud for sleeping ears). My kids are sweet and allow me to rouse them from their slumber. Then my husband and I watch as our kids open up their stockings and gifts, loving each squeal, smile and thank you!

The Bible says in Matthew 7:11, "If you, then, though you are evil, know how to give good gifts to your children, how much more will your Father in heaven give good gifts to those who ask him!" Jesus isn't calling us evil, He's just saying in comparison to our perfect, holy, Heavenly Father we can't come close to being as good as He is. And yet… we know how to give good things to our kids, so how much more does HE want to give us good things? He loves us and says He wants to do good to us, not to harm us. I pray that each one of us will see that we truly have a good and loving God. I just think about myself laying there wide awake waiting for my kids to wake up, how much more my loving Father? I pray that we will know the great love that the Father has for us!

Ordinary People

Margie McCready

Exodus 4:13 But Moses said, "Pardon your servant, Lord. Please send someone else."

I had just recently moved back to the country with my 2 year old twin daughters, Rachel and Melanie. It was not a choice I had made on my own. I was determined to make a good life for my girls and do the best I could to reassure them on a daily basis that they were secure and loved. It was my third day there and I was gazing out the window in deep thought. All of a sudden I observed a white haired, little toddler running with all his might up the street. Close behind him was a very distraught woman trying to catch him. I was amused for a few seconds until I realized the gap between them was growing. She was not going to catch him and he was headed for a busy intersection. I bolted out my front door and flew in their direction. I said "Hi" to the woman as I passed her and caught up to the little guy in time. He laughed with all his might when I picked him up….until he realized that I was not his mother. He let out a scream which I immediately responded to and deposited him in his mother's arms. She was breathless and couldn't speak. She didn't need to. Her eyes said it all. That was my first encounter with my new neighbor, Annie.

I soon discovered about the only thing we had in common was our 2 year old children. She was a very devout Catholic and didn't want to hear anything about the Jesus I tried to share with her. She was not interested. It was a closed door. For months I just kept reaching out and loving her, and holding up the cup of "Living Water." One night it happened. She took the cup and she received Jesus as her Savior. What a marvelous transformation took place that night! She was never the same. That was 35 years ago. She is one of my closest Christian friends and loves the Lord with all her heart. She has affected many lives for Jesus. We meet one day a week and pray together. We have seen miracles take place on a regular basis.

God uses ordinary people. As flawed as we are, He chooses to dwell in us and touch other lives through us. We are His representatives on this earth. We are His hands, His feet, His voice. We cannot and must not be silent. The world is thirsty and Jesus is the only one who can quench their thirst. It is up to us to offer them the cup. They may not take it. That is not our responsibility. We must offer it and then leave the results to God. It can be risky. It isn't easy. Sometimes the water is thrown back in our face. But for the one who receives it, they will never be the same.

We are called to love. There are certain people the Lord wants to reach through you and I. He will direct our paths to cross and then impart to us the wisdom and guidance to make it happen. It is divine love in action. God works in mysterious ways, His wonders to perform. Little did Annie and I know that we had a divine appointment that day on a road called Muncie Avenue. How thankful I am that I had my running shoes on!

Sky Hike

Jennifer Knox

*Isaiah 41:10 So do not fear, for I am with you;
do not be dismayed, for I am your God, I will
strengthen you and help you; I will uphold you
with my righteous right hand.*

I have never really been a big fan of heights. In my
opinion, if God had wanted us up that high, he would
have made us birds. If one was to look closely, which
I have, one would notice the absence of wings on we
humans. Thus bringing me back to my point, heights
are for flying creatures, the ground for people... that
is unless you are attempting the Stone Mountain,
Georgia "Sky Hike!"

Even though I don't particularly like heights, I
was completely enjoying the Sky Hike. It's a ropes
course that takes place forty feet in the air. For anyone
who has wanted to be a tight rope walker, this is
their chance! It's completely safe, since everyone is

harnessed to a security beam overhead. The entire maze of ropes takes about an hour to complete, but is filled with excitement, laughter and fun. I was having a great time laughing, smiling and cheering each person on... oh, did I mention I was on the ground watching? I had no intention of getting on the thing! Although, I must admit it looked fairly easy since my own children, niece and nephew were maneuvering their way around it with no problem.

As each family member passed over my perch (which was on the ground), I would snap pictures, cheer them on and spur them to go faster. At one point, my husband came into view and I noticed he was walking a narrow plank without holding on to his harness. There's no need to hold on to it, since it is secured around each person's legs and torso. He had his hands straight out to his sides for balance and carefully took each step. Now, from where I was, it looked easy! "C'mon babe! You can go faster than that!" He didn't give me much attention since he was focused on the task at hand. I sat there wondering why he didn't try running the thing, maybe even do a gymnastics jump split... you know that move where they jump and do a split in the air and land safely on the beam. All of a sudden I was lost in Olympic world and could picture myself as Mary Lou Retton sticking the landing on one of those beams or ropes above my head. But, alas, someone had to stay on the ground to watch the cameras, wallets and purses. My inner Mary Lou Retton would have to settle for cheering from the sidelines.

That was until my sister came bolting up to me, "Jen, come on, we've got ten minutes, let's go do just a part of the ropes course!" A moment ago I was ready to win the Sky Hike Olympic Gold, but sanity was quickly returning to me, I don't like heights! But it was too late, as any younger sibling knows... when the older one tells you to do something, you do it. I seem to forget the fact that I'm almost forty years old and have now outgrown my sister by three inches! Nevertheless, she is the big sister, and I must do as commanded!

Before I knew what was happening I was being harnessed, tethered, tied, wrapped and launched into the great unknown. Since we only had ten minutes, my sister had the great idea that we'd skip the first two levels and ascend the stairs to level three. I was caught up in the moment and feeling good about the whole thing since I had become an expert watching from below... this would be easy! As we headed from the safety of the stairwell reality came into focus, we are walking on ropes in the air! There are no safety nets under us! I could instantly feel my neck getting hot and my vision was starting to blur. My sister took a glance back at me to make sure I was ready for the leap, when she saw that familiar look in my eye... "Jen, are you ok?" She knew! I had no choice but to move forward, there is no going back on this ride. The line piles up behind each person, and the safety cords can only go forward!

I locked my gaze straight ahead and somehow I made it across the first portion of the maze. It wasn't too bad, as this was the plank walk, ahead of me was the rope walk! I stood on the waiting platform for the next part of our maze. My hands were sweaty and losing their grip on the safety harness over my head, but I just held on all the tighter. I watched as little kids giggled their way across the rope, all the while dreading my turn. Then, it was upon me! I stood staring at the rope I was to walk on, with people below me looking like little ants! Then I noticed one of the little ants was filming me! It was my husband! I gave a quick glare in his direction at the thought of this being recorded for all of time. My sister was cheering me on telling me I could do it, but my feet were glued to the platform. I tried to make them move, but they have learned that they were created for solid ground, not moving ropes suspended miles above the ground (well, maybe not miles… but off the ground nonetheless!).

My mind was racing at the thought that I had allowed my children, my precious children to walk across this thing! Had I lost my mind? I had encouraged them to go faster and let go! I must have read too many books on how to empower your children, I needed to focus more on the books of how to instill wisdom into those you love! But I couldn't think about that right now, I had to find a way off this thing! Maybe they could just bring me a ladder? I'm not sure how much time had passed, but enough that the safety guide was making his way over to me. The line was building behind me, and it was his job to make the scared line holder uppers move! "Ma'am, you're ok." I looked up to see a young teenage boy trying to lure me out onto the rope. I immediately resented the word Ma'am. "The first step is the hardest," he urged me on. I know the first step is the hardest! I pushed out four children… don't talk to me about hard! Now, I'm not sure why we moms like to revert back to our birthing experiences to validate ourselves, but it just seems to justify many of our actions.

By now the line was growing, the camera was rolling and my sister and Mr. Teenager were encouraging me off into the danger zone. Somehow, and I don't know how, but my foot disobeyed everything I've ever taught it, and it stepped onto the rope. The rope swayed and bent, but even still, on went my next foot. Now I was committed, there was no stopping, unless I wanted to watch my children get married from atop this ropes course! My sister stood in front of me cheering and supporting me, I think my husband would have, but didn't want to admit to the public that this woman was his. Then it happened! The dreaded, horrible, humiliating... tears! Yes! Tears! Tears in front of teenage "Ma'am" guy! Tears in front of crowds of ant people! Tears in front of the camera! My sister overlooked her own shame of being related to me and cheered me on all the more. As I made the final step onto the podium (not the Olympic podium I had dreamed of earlier) I was greeted with my sister's applause and affirming words, "I'm so proud of you Jen! You did it!" Even Mr. Teenager seemed proud that he had got me to walk the rope of horror! I immediately asked if there was any way off this thing, and to my GREAT delight there was an exit. I took myself down that thing as fast as I could and set my feet back on the ground they were made for... all the while... the camera rolled!

I wiped the tears off my face and yanked those safety harnesses off of me and was finally returning back to life the way it should be. Flat. Safe. Happy! It was over! Then I started thinking, what was that all about? Did I really just cry on a ropes course? Why was I so scared? My little niece who is eight did this thing! Then it hit me, I didn't trust the harness.

Isn't that what faith in God is like? Life really isn't a whole lot different from that ropes course. It's unknown, adventurous, unstable, exhilarating and at times can be scary… but do you trust the harness? Do you trust the One who holds you? I realized we all are on the ride of life, but those who trust the harness enjoy it all the more! The greater our faith in God's ability to keep us safe through all of life's uncertainty, bumps and frailties, the greater our peace through it all. Some will learn to trust, some will never trust. Some will let go and enjoy the thrill, others will cling in fear. I for one, want to love the life God gave me, knowing He is the ultimate safety harness. His word is true when He said in Isaiah 41:10, "So do not fear, for I am with you; do not be dismayed, for I am your God, I will strengthen you and help you; I will uphold you with my righteous right hand." I pray each one of us will be able to walk boldly through life knowing God is holding tight to us!

Put a Lid on the Attitude or You may Just Find a Stocking

Patty Knox

Proverbs 16:17a The highway of the upright avoids trouble.

I've mentioned my hubby, Bob, in several of my articles, because after all, our lives have been intertwined now for forty-two years and counting. We have led a full life together so full that it has included blissful, bountiful (four children and seventeen grandchildren), wonderful, delightful, and all the positive "fulls" you can think of to add to matrimony. Then there is the flip side of full to every marriage made in Heaven. You know, the thunder and lightning side, like stressful and painful, even, JUST ABOUT HAD IT UP TO HERE FULL! This is cousin to HAD A BELLY FULL! Now, Noah Webster mentions nothing in his dictionary about the last two phrases mentioned, but anyone who has walked down the aisle knows better right? Besides, either our good friend Noah wasn't married or his book is outdated. After all, a lot of new words have been introduced since 1828! Especially in my family, because we make up new words when the old ones don't seem to fit. If it makes sense to us, we use it!

I would like to relate to you an experience that my better half and I had early on in our marriage that put "just about had it up to here full" in the dictionary. The year was 1971, one year after Bob and myself tied the knot. I was nineteen and already quite skilled in the sport of spousal sparring. If I was upset at my husband, I would bring out the weapon of warfare that could best remedy the situation and place me in the winner's circle....or so I thought, until Bob offered up a sucker punch that landed a stocking cap over my entire face! Allow me to explain the events that led to this humiliation I suffered brought on by my own stubbornness.

First of all, I was nineteen, a fact that most likely helped lend itself to my foolish and immature behavior. This, I acknowledge, was no excuse for my stinky attitude, but I'm sure it did help contribute to my husband defaulting to his only weapon of self defense at the moment.

We had traded in my cool blue and silver 1959 Chevy with side fins that looked like two giant wasp wings. I loved that gas hog. So what if it took up two lanes on the road and was a pain to maneuver in downtown Seattle traffic? So what if we burned some of the tread off the tires every time we had to yield at the top of a hill? So what if it jerked and leaped forward at every red light due to the manual stick shift and clutch pedal? I loved that beast! Bob, on the other hand had, reached his limit, had his BELLY FULL and traded old faithful to a friend of his for the scrappiest Volkswagen bug that ever inched its way out onto the highway. It was several different colors due to donated parts, did not have a working heater or defrost system so we had to manually scrape the inside of the windows when the weather turned cold, and the list could go on. However, in Bob's eyes, that ugly pup was great on gas! Gas being at that time a whopping twenty-seven cents per gallon!

During this early season of wedded bliss, Bob was finishing his last nine months in the service at Fort Lewis, Washington, and we were staying with his parents in Seattle, but traveling on weekends to Quilcene, my home town, about two hours away on the Olympic Peninsula. This is where I had met and married Bob in a small church in town and where he was still helping to minister in on Sundays. Because of the distance traveled every weekend, little ugly was the best solution for making the trips back and forth, since it was cheaper on the gas tank. The problem was, little ugly started to have little breakdowns. Then came the day when that slug bug left us stranded in Quilcene on a Sunday afternoon. Now, when you have to report to Uncle Sam on Monday morning, you don't just call in sick or take a day of vacation. So we were left in a real dilemma, until a friend in the church with a truck offered to tow us with a "chain" ninety miles over open highways which included boarding a ferry only to be dumped off at the downtown Seattle waterfront. Now, let me enlighten you on the difference between a chain tow and a tow bar, just in case you are not familiar with the two. With a tow bar, one does not actually have to ride in and steer the junk heap that is being towed!

Well, Bob saw the guy's offer as an answer to prayer and a great idea, and let's just say I did not bear witness to the idea at all, and wasn't so sure it was an answer to prayer either when I eyeballed the friend's truck with bald tires and old rusty chain. Let me tell you, I tried every trick in the book to "snaggle" (family word here not found in Noah's library) my way out of that trip back. My logical conclusion was to stay behind at my folk's until little ugly bug was up and running! Now that I think back, Bob was probably resistant to that idea because he knew deep inside that this gas saver was a piece of junk and beyond repairs and he was afraid he wouldn't have a vehicle to come back in to rescue his bride.

I don't know for sure if this was his reasoning, but I do know that he somehow talked me into the front seat of that broken down Volkswagen bug and we jerked our way behind an old pickup with a chain attached to the front bumper. After several whiplashes, which transpired before we even got on to the open highway, my blood started to boil. I was irritated and nettled thinking that I had agreed to such a ridiculous, not to mention dangerous, expedition. About half an hour into the tow journey, my hubby could see the steam coming out of my ears as my blood was now starting to boil over, forming a thick fog on the windshield, and since the defroster was broken and he didn't have a rag handy, he decided to try and make small talk to clear the air. It was then that I chose my weapon of defense! Silence! Absolute, complete 'you do not exist and I am not here either' kind of silence!

Those who know my Bob know that he really is one of the most kind and patient people on the planet, so he tried coaxing me out of my foul attitude for miles down the highway to no avail.

Finally, about thirty miles from our destination, I could tell his patience was being tested to the max. *Good*, I thought to my selfish self, *my weapon of choice is working*. I was hoping it would kick in before arriving home. Then he tried for the last time to diffuse the silence by pointing out a house off to the left that was made to look like a castle. I quickly looked away to show my complete absence from the scenery and the present company before me and that's when out of nowhere a gold stocking cap with green stripes around the edge that looked identical to the one my hubby was wearing at the time was stuffed completely over my head, face and all, all the way down to my neck!

My first reaction was complete disbelief. My second reaction was "stink!" my weapon of silence must have malfunctioned leaving me open to attack. My third reaction which I chose to give in to was ugly, ugly, pride! How did I know it was pride? Because I left that stocking cap stuffed over my face for miles! I cringe now just thinking how much enjoyment it must have brought to passerby's out on the highway. And who knows the story that circulated back at the church by the guy towing us who got a play by play of the whole unfolding drama from his rear view mirror. Plus, even though Bob would never admit it, I'm certain he too drew some compensation out of his traveling sidekick's comedy act. My only sick satisfaction gained from that whole episode was the cold, red ears Bob was sporting when I finally decided to remove that stocking cap and return it to its rightful owner. Now just a little side note here, I've read in Proverbs about men going to the corner of a house top to get away from an annoying wife, but I've yet to find in the scriptures where a gold stocking cap with green stripes substitutes for that! But, in all honesty, I was in the wrong and take full responsibility for my trouble making attitude.

Thank goodness I have a forgiving husband who through the years has manifested (for the most part) yielding patience, forgiveness, long suffering, kindness and gentleness when I least deserved it. I once ruined all the windows on the back of our house and I panicked! Bob calmly replied that they were just windows and could be replaced. What husband says that when he is seeing dollar signs flash before his eyes?

Bob would be the first to tell you he is far from perfect, especially if I happen to vex him when he's wearing a certain stocking cap. Myself? Well I'm still far from perfect, but I am realizing that like the scripture states in Proverbs, the highway of the upright avoids trouble. Plus, I've come to the conclusion that there should have been a chapter in the good book devoted to men like my husband, similar to the chapter in Proverbs 31 that is devoted to Godly women. If there was, I'm sure it would read something along these lines:

A man of noble character who can find? He is worth far more than a new car. His wife has full confidence in him. He brings her good and not harm on the highway of life that they share together. He speaks with kindness and wisdom when his wife of aging years sets scratches to his windows. He prays and watches over the affairs of his household. His children arise and call him blessed. His grandchildren arise and call him Grandpa. His wife also praises him. Many men do noble things but you surpass them all. Ego is deceptive and muscles are fleeting; but the man who fears the Lord is to be praised.

That's my husband, and if you look close I'll just bet you will find some of the finger prints of your husband there also.

The Bible teaches us women to honor and respect our men. Not because they are perfect, but because it pleases our Heavenly Father, and might I add, it helps to keep us upright and out of trouble! So remember dear ones, when you're out and about with your better half, keep a good attitude so you won't have to look foolish in someone else's stocking cap.

The Standing Ovation

Margie McCready

Matthew 25:23 His master replied, "Well done, good and faithful servant! You have been faithful with a few things; I will put you in charge of many things. Come and share your master's happiness!"

The crowd rose to their feet and the applause was deafening. I loved it. I swelled with pride as I watched my three daughters, Corinne, Heather and Hillary bow and beam with delight. They had worked very hard for many months and they deserved the praise they were receiving. All those years of shuffling them to dance classes had paid off. This was the fruit of that seed planted many years ago, before they were even old enough to go to school. Now, years later, all three of them had landed parts in the famous Christmas play "The Nutcracker". I was thrilled. The performance was beyond anything I could ever have imagined. The costumes were over the top. It was one of the most exciting nights of my life and it will be forever etched in my memory. I asked them after we had driven home what it was like to receive a standing ovation from the crowd. Not one of them could put the experience into words...there just weren't any.

I personally have never received a standing ovation, and maybe you haven't either. Some of us just aren't privy to it, at least not in this life. I have a wonderful surprise for you! One day you and I will hear applause, but it will not be man's applause. It will be the applause of Heaven. We will stand before our precious Savior and hear His words spoken to us personally. "Well done." Those who have served Him humbly and patiently in this life will receive their due reward. He will notice and He will applaud! Can you imagine? Receiving a standing ovation from the Creator of the universe, the King of all Kings, and Lord of all Lords? The one who owns it all and yet gave His all for us with no regrets? The one to whom we owe our very life?

Like my daughters, there will be no words to describe our gratefulness...we will just do what they did that night and bow...and lay our crowns at His feet.

The applause of God is all that matters.

A Penny for your Thoughts

Patty Knox

Numbers 32:23 You may be sure that your sin will find you out.

I never would have guessed that the above scripture would find me out forty four years after graduating from High School, but it certainly did when I decided to head back to my home town of Quilcene, Washington to attend a fair that they sponsor every September.

I enjoyed seeing the parade and being in the town group photo for the local newspaper. My sister and I decided to walk the halls of our elementary school and reminisce about teachers and former classmates. Then we headed over to the cafeteria to grab a bite of lunch. It was here that we bumped into a former high school teacher who greeted us with a smile and opened her conversation by reminding us that her husband (also our former teacher) still told the story about a student who hit him in the head with a penny!

My face instantly turned fire engine red while my eyebrows lifted themselves to the top of my head! I suddenly began to relive that moment in my tenth grade Current Events class when Mr. Bennett caught me and another classmate playing poker.

I know I should have been taking notes and paying attention to what was being said in the front of the class, but current events that didn't involve my life at the present were just not worth taking notes over. Sitting in the back of the class however, and playing cards was on my radar of current happenings.

Doug would shuffle the cards quietly in his lap and sneak five over to me and the game was on. We played for money too! Pennies sat in a pile atop our desks waiting to be added to or subtracted from (at least we were sharpening our math skills).

On this particular day I was on a winning streak as hand after hand my mountain of pennies grew. I was so engrossed in my cards that I failed to hear the cough signal being passed down the aisle that warned of impending danger. That's when Mr. Bennett swooped in and nabbed my cards, disrupting another potential winning hand. He turned and advanced back up the aisle toward his desk.

This is when my spontaneous (okay, compulsive side) came out and I tossed a penny from my desk to the front of the room just as Mr. Bennett turned around to face the class and that coin pegged him right between the eyes. I don't think David could have aimed better when dealing with Goliath!

I honestly never intended to hit Mr Bennett, I was just "throwing" off steam. To make matters worse he saw the heap of pennies on my desk so he knew who had fired the weapon. How do you smooth that one over? Well, I didn't and found myself in the principal's office. I had to serve detention but thankfully my teacher allowed me to return to class even though he wore a penny imprint on his forehead for a day or so.

Mrs. Bennett assured me that day in the cafeteria that all was well and her husband actually enjoyed retelling the story about being showered with money by a student. *Great,* I thought, *my sin had been passed around for years.* Here I stood, forty five years later, repenting to my teacher via his wife who promised to relay the message.

I realized an important truth from this encounter with Mrs. Bennett. Some of the bad decisions we have made in the past can leave a negative imprint on others. Yes, Mr. Bennett was gracious and forgiving toward me, however, what about past damaging choices we have made that truly offended someone causing them to carry unsettled memories for years when we assume they have forgotten? There's a penny for your thoughts, huh?

Or, what about past sins that we ourselves have not taken ownership of and repented for? The Bible says that they will surely find us out. If I would have taken notes in class instead of playing cards I would not have been called out on my transgression forty five years later and certainly would have saved myself an embarrassing moment! But bringing it to light gave me the opportunity to clear the air of flying pennies.

How about you? Are there things in your past that you have tucked away, tried to forget and hope others have too? Allow me to humbly offer some advice. Bring this baggage out into the light and place it before the Lord Jesus. Ask for forgiveness and extend forgiveness graciously to others as well. Then with head held high and your pocket full of pennies, enjoy that country fair of yours without fear of "your sins finding you out!" I know I will this coming September.

God's Mouse Piece

Jennifer Knox

Ephesians 6:19-20 Pray also for me, that whenever I speak, words may be given me so that I will fearlessly make known the mystery of the gospel, for which I am an ambassador in chains. Pray that I may declare it fearlessly, as I should.

"You are God's mouse piece!" Those were the words I was hearing as a sweet lady was praying for me. Again and again she said, "Yes! You are God's mouse piece! You are God's mouse piece!" What does it mean to be God's mouse piece? I once had a mouse in my house, and it was not a happy moment! Actually, if truth be told, I have had many mice… and rats (much worse in my opinion, than a mouse) in my house! As her words rang in my ears, my mind traveled to the mouse that I found in my one year old's hands!

I was still relatively new at the whole mom thing when this particular day happened. It was early morning when I set my ten month old, Faith, on the floor to play in her room while I brushed my teeth. When I finished, I looked into her room to see what she was doing. I was a little perplexed at the toy she had in her hand. I had only been gone for two minutes (the prescribed amount of time for proper oral hygiene). The little "toy" flopped back and forth as she twisted her little wrist back and forth. As I got closer to see what it was, I was absolutely horrified at my findings! My beloved, innocent, CLEAN, little baby was holding a DIRTY DEAD MOUSE! Yes! Yes! Yes! A dead mouse in my baby's hand!

I scooped up my daughter, smashed the dead mouse with a toy (just to make sure it was dead) and immediately ran to the phone to call poison control. I was fearful to tell them what was going on for fear they kept a "bad mother journal" that can and will be used against me. Nevertheless, I told them what had happened and was surprised when they had a plan for such a case. Had other mothers called about dead mice in their child's hand before? I was starting to feel somewhat better about the situation. The man on the phone instructed me to put her in the bath right away and give her a bottle of milk to flush out her system. WHAT?! Flush out her system?! That would imply that the DIRTY DEAD MOUSE had been in her mouth! My mind hadn't even gone there! Horrified, I plopped my baby in the tub with a warm bottle of milk. She thought the whole thing was quite fun, as she loved nothing better than baths and bottles. I, on the other hand, was furious at my husband! What does my husband have to do with this, you ask? Nothing! But at that moment, I needed someone to blame and so it was him for moving us into this house! My poor husband, he has been so patient with me.

The words, "You are God's mouse piece!" interrupted my daydreaming of days gone by, and I was brought back to the woman's prayer. "You are God's mouse piece." It was then that I realized she wasn't saying "mouse piece," but "MOUTH piece!" Ohhhh... I was God's mouthpiece! As she finished praying for me, I pondered her words. What does it mean to be God's mouthpiece? I looked back on times in my life when I was more of a timid mouse than a bold mouth! It got me thinking about reasons why I was timid. I didn't want to offend anyone. I didn't want to hurt anyone. I didn't want anyone to be mad at me.

So I ask this question to you and to myself... why would we be a "mouse" (aka: timid) piece instead of a "mouth" piece for God? The word "gospel" means "good news." Jesus came to this world not to condemn the world, but to save the world! He is full of mercy, kindness, love, and compassion. This is really good news! I know so many people who are hurting. They are dealing with all kinds of struggles and trials... huge things... things like a cheating spouse, children dying from drugs, loved ones dying from cancer, financial ruin... big, big things. If I am God's mouthpiece, then I am here to tell them that God loves them. God is for them. God is not mad at them. God knows them. Sometimes just knowing that God knows you and what you are going through is all you need to keep standing. God may not always fix the situation the way you want Him to... but He will always walk with you.

On my darkest day, when I felt that I could not go on, I remember what kept me going. It wasn't my finances. It wasn't my husband. It wasn't my kids. It was God. I remember it like it was yesterday. As I laid on the floor with tears pouring down my cheeks I asked for my Bible. I could barely breath at that moment. My mouth was so dry from shock that I needed water to be able swallow. My entire body was numb and trembling with adrenaline and fear. I didn't know what the future held for me, but I knew one thing... Jesus. I clutched onto my Bible with all that was in me. I wrapped my arms around it, slept with it, cried into it... I placed all my hope into the words of that book. The Bible became my everything because they were the very words of God.

How many people are having their darkest day today? How many people are numb with fear and anxiety? The words of Jesus are what will give them hope and life. How could I ever withhold that from them? How could I ever be anything more than the mouthpiece of God's goodness and love? I'm sure you know people who need words of life and hope. So my question to you is the same one I've asked myself... are you going to be God's mouse piece... timid and shy? Or God's mouthpiece... bold and full of life?

Sometimes We Just Need to See a Rainbow

Patty Knox

Genesis 9:16 Whenever the rainbow appears in the clouds I will see it and remember the everlasting covenant between God and all living creatures of every kind on earth.

When life brings us sorrow from losing a loved one it can be extremely hard to look beyond the grief that surrounds us. This past year in my family, we lost a number of family members and friends. It seemed to happen like a domino effect, or better yet an avalanche that invaded our lives and left our hearts saddened.

My dear sister Karen, still in her sixties, had a massive stroke that ended her life fourteen days later. "Gub" as we called her, was ready to meet Jesus, being a strong and loving Christian. Also, being a widow for several years and living alone, she now longed for

Heaven's gates and got her wish sooner than later but it didn't make it any easier for us left behind.

On the day of Karen's funeral we received a call on the way to the graveside service telling us that my father-in-law Bill had just passed away. Just moments before that, we received the news that my daughter-in-law had just experienced a miscarriage. In the two months that followed, my son-in-law Scott laid his dear mother to rest, while a close friend of mine unexpectedly lost her husband.

Talk about grief and sorrow. We were experiencing it for a number of loved ones all at the same time. We traveled from one funeral to the next. It felt like a dark, black cloud had settled over our lives during that time.

Grief has a way of dampening our thoughts and emotions, not to mention our faith. If we do not properly work through that grief and look beyond the grave we may begin to doubt God's goodness and faithfulness. Allow me give you an example.

There is a story in the bible in John chapter 11 that speaks about a friend of Jesus whose name was Lazareth. Lazareth's two sisters sent for Jesus one day to come and heal their brother when he was sick, but according to their assessment Jesus didn't show concern when he chose to delay and their brother died. When Jesus finally arrived Lazareth had been in a tomb for three days and the sisters were distraught. They cried out "master if you would have been here sooner our brother would not have died." Well, the truth is Jesus was right on time and Lazareth was called by name back to life.

For the Christians that have gone on before us, Jesus has called them by name and believe me when I say that they could not be more alive. Jesus also proclaimed that in his Father's house (meaning Heaven) were many mansions and that Jesus himself was going ahead of us to prepare them for us. I guess you could call that a rainbow promise. Sometimes though, we just need to see the rainbow to remember God's promises to us and our loved ones. Mary and Martha, the sisters of Lazareth, failed to see not only the rainbow of hope that Jesus promised but also that he was indeed the fulfillment of that rainbow. He was the resurrection and the life!

Gub's rainbow was evident by the hope she carried in her heart, that someday she would cross Heaven's threshold without a limp and run into the everlasting arms of the Lord whom she loved so much. Karen was never able to run in this life because of physical limitations, but her rainbow's end assures me that she is home now, probably running laps around her mansion!

My father-in-law's rainbow showed up in stunning colors when at an old age Billy happily surrendered his life to Christ. It took a long time for him to find his rainbow of hope and peace. Funny how a rainbow can be in plain sight and yet we can refuse to see the promises attached to it. To choose living under a rain cloud with a dark umbrella over our heads when a beautiful, colorful life is right above us. I'm thankful Billy chose to fold up that umbrella and catch sight of his rainbow.

Sweet Jeaniene, my son-in-law's mother. She suffered much in her body from a terminal illness, yet her promised rainbow filled up the entire sky when the angels ushered her over that colored arch and into the arms of her Savior. Her body, now free from pain, cashed in on its rainbow and who knows? she may be running laps with my sister Gub, or swimming in the river of life, as she loved water. Or being the incredible artist that she was living here, perhaps she is painting with exquisite colors up there, colors that would seem drab and pale to her now if she were back here on earth. My friend Debbie, who said goodbye to her husband found her rainbow in the assurance that

Marty had rededicated his life to the one who now offered him eternal life.

I'm just wondering, if maybe in our hard times and painful moments, we just need to look around to find our promised rainbow. It may not always show up in the sky but I believe God has a rainbow for each one of us. Do you need to see a rainbow today? We would be wise to remember that a rainbow will never appear without the rain and the sun. Through the good times and bad the Lord wants us to know that He will faithfully keep His promises to us. We are not always offered a life without pain and suffering while living here on earth but the beautiful rainbow's display of hope with its eternal colors of promise can makes it well worth the journey! Yes indeed, God has promised all of us a rainbow. Are you looking for yours? Look close, you just might find it in the most unexpected place.

Secret Snacks

Jennifer Knox

Proverbs 9:17-18 "Stolen water is sweet; food eaten in secret is delicious!" But little do they know that the dead are there, that her guests are deep in the realm of the dead.

Have you ever noticed that kids eat all day long? It never ceased to amaze me how much of my day was consumed with feeding my four children when they were small. I would wonder how someone so small could consume so much. Our days consisted of waking up, eating breakfast, cleaning up from breakfast, eating a snack, cleaning after the snack, eating lunch, cleaning after lunch, eating a snack, cleaning, dinner, cleaning, snack, cleaning... bed! Then the next day arrived and the cycle continued. Food consumed our days.

I had been aware of the fact that I lived most of my life in the kitchen, but it never hit me to such a great extent as when I went on my first fast. Our church group had decided to go on a forty day fast that would entail only eating dinner. I was eager to have this time set apart to draw closer to God and spend more time in His Word and in prayer. I had great visions of a glorious forty days with just me and Jesus!

The fast was going great and I was feeling closer to God and not even a bit hungry... until breakfast the first day of the fast! As I stood there making my kids their hot cereal, I salivated as I looked at that package of dry mush being poured into the bowl of hot water. I didn't even eat breakfast on most days, but this day was different, I COULD'T have breakfast! Now all I could think of was breakfast! Then came the snack, then lunch, then the snack, and so on. My hunger was dominating my every moment.

As the weeks dragged on, my hunger only seemed to intensify. I lived from morning to night hungry, and not for more of God (as I thought would happen) but hungry for anything and everything! The only reprieve came at dinner and that only satisfied for a few short hours and the hunger would return. I found myself sitting over bowls of boxed macaroni and cheese sniffing it to try and trick myself into believing that I was eating it.

Finally, after several weeks of misery, and feeling no closer to God, I decided it was time for me to call it quits! The whole point of the fast was to spend more time with God, and all I was doing was spending time lamenting over not eating! Breaking the fast left me in a bit of a quandary though, I didn't want to discourage the others in our group from continuing on with the fast. I came up with the brilliant plan of eating in secret! I would break the fast, but I wouldn't tell anyone. My intention wasn't to deceive anyone, I just didn't want to be a hinderance to them.

I felt a wave of freedom as I sat down to enjoy my first lunch in almost a month, but something inside me was nagging at me. I was thinking about something a friend had said to me once, "The Lord speaks when you open His Word, and when you close the book, He closes His mouth." Now, I'm not saying that is doctrinally sound, since the Lord can speak to us in many ways, but it did give me the idea to "try" and see if the Lord had anything He wanted to tell me before I dove into my secret lunch.

I did one of those things that people say never to do, but most of us have done... I prayed, "Lord, if you want to say anything to me about breaking this fast, please do it through the verse I turn to." Then I flopped open my Bible, pointed my finger to a scripture, and read what it said. I can tell you, what I saw left me dumbfounded! I turned straight to Proverbs 9:17-18 "Stolen water is sweet; food eaten in secret is delicious! But little do they know that the dead are there, that her guests are deep in the realm of the dead." I could not believe that I would have read anything about eating food in secret, nor did I even know that there was such a verse in the entire Bible. Needless to say, I did NOT eat lunch that day, nor did I break my fast!

What I learned from that experience had nothing to do with eating or not eating. It had nothing to do with keeping secrets or exposing myself. What I learned from it was I have a God who knows me! I've tried this "flip the Bible open and point" many times since and it has been far less effective, but I still can't forget the moment when He really did speak to me that way. As I've matured in my walk with God, I've found that as I daily seek Him, He has been so faithful to lead me in the way I should go. His Word has taken root in my life and has kept me from going places and doing things that He knows are not for my best. If we will take the time, He really will speak to us in His still and gentle voice.

The Day the White House Called

Margie McCready

Jeremiah 33:3 Call to me and I will answer you and tell you great and unsearchable things you do not know.

It was a beautiful morning. I had just returned home from running some errands and decided to check my caller ID. I was waiting to hear from my husband, Mark, who works for Alaska Power & Telephone. He had left the day before on a business trip to Sitka. He travels to remote places where phone service is hindered, but I knew he would call as soon as he was able.

While scrolling through the caller ID on my phone to see who had called while I was out, a name jumped out at me. At first I thought I wasn't seeing the name correctly, but sure enough in big bold capital letters it read, 'The White House.' The number that followed was unfamiliar to me. My heart jumped. Why is someone from the White House calling our home? My mind immediately began racing. I was in a state of shock for a few minutes as multiple scenarios played out in my mind. Whatever the reason, I knew it had to be extremely important.

Our answering machine was clearly turned on but they did not leave a message. I assumed it was too important a matter, and they needed to speak in person. I was feeling very singled out and excited. I had to tell someone! I started with calling my daughters, but it didn't stop there, as I began calling all of my friends. I couldn't wait to let everyone else in on my excitement. Their response was all the same, "No way, are you serious?! Let me know as soon as you hear back from them." One friend even said, "Maybe you were nominated for something special and they are going to fly you to Washington DC as a surprise."

My curiosity swelled, as well as my head. I hung around in my house for the remainder of the day just waiting for the phone to ring. Every time it did, I jumped. Finally at 8pm the call came through. Sure enough, there it was flashing on my caller ID 'The White House.' I felt like I was going to faint. My heart was pounding in my chest as I picked up the phone and answered in my best voice, "Hello?" I then heard a voice say, "Hey Hon, how are you?" I was speechless. Who from the White House would be calling me Hon? I responded, "Who is this?" To which the voice said, "What?" I felt like I was in the Twilight Zone. Then I heard, "Honey, are you ok?" This person sounded EXACTLY like my husband. "Mark?" I said. "Yes, who did you think it was?" he responded. I certainly wasn't going to tell him, only The President. "What on earth are you doing in Washington DC?!" I asked. "What are you talking about? I am in Sitka." He said. "Sitka, Alaska? The caller ID shows that you are calling from The White House." I responded. There was a long pause, followed by immediate laughter on the other end. The laughter went on a little too long for my comfort. "Oh that!" He said, "I am staying at a large Bed & Breakfast that is painted all white, and they named it 'The White House' for fun." The joke was on me.

I felt like a balloon when you let all the air out. I was humiliated. Then I had remembered everyone I had called earlier! How would I ever live this down?! I didn't answer the phone the rest of the night. The next day I went shopping for hours, anything to stay away from the phone ringing. I had a lot of messages when I returned home, as I expected, everyone was curious as to what happened with the White House situation. When I was finally confronted with nowhere to run,

I told them, "Yes, the White House did call back, but it was a wrong number." I chose to leave the name on the caller ID just to show my kids that The White House really did call me. In fact, I didn't erase it for a very long time. Every time I looked at it, I smiled...and wondered what I would have said if it really would have been the President of the United States. One thing I know for sure that I wouldn't have said was, "I didn't vote for you."

The Glory Seat

Margie McCready

Psalm 77:14 You are the God who performs miracles; you display your power among the peoples.

I headed into the stadium to watch my grandson, Berkley Hill play football. He is the quarterback for the Port Townsend High School Redskins team. He is #11. He has been given the nickname 'Crazy Legs Hill' because he is fast, very fast. He can maneuver on the field where his legs are going in every direction.

My daughter Rachel, Berkley's mom, had arrived early to save our seats. As I scanned the stadium, I didn't see her, but I did see my Granddaughter Lane, who is a Cheerleader for the Redskins, and also Berkley's sister. "Is your mom here?" I asked her. "Yes." She said, "But she had to leave for a minute. Her gray blanket is right up there, and you will see her other things." I looked up to where Lane was pointing and that is when I noticed the man I would be sitting next to. I had not seen him in years. I was thrilled! His wife Bethany was sitting next to him. As we exchanged our hellos, I noticed how radiant and healthy he looked. Not one trace of the cancer that had ravaged his body and nearly took his life years earlier.

When Mark and I met Paul, he was just a teenager in our youth group, at Peninsula Christian Fellowship. We were his youth leaders. Paul was very keen on a pretty little brunette who was also in our youth group, named Bethany. A young romance ensued and they would eventually marry. In the years following, they had two sons, Johnathan and David. Then came the horrible news. Paul was diagnosed with pancreatic cancer and given a 5% chance to live. His boys were very small. His bride was devastated. The doctors told her to get things in order for his death. She refused. She refused to accept their diagnosis and she earnestly sought the Lord for a miracle. It would take a miracle. It looked hopeless, his weight had dropped to the point where he was almost unrecognizable. Bethany never gave up hope. She prayed and prayed and prayed, and believed God. She said, "I need my husband, and my boys need their father." I was amazed and astounded at her tenacity. She refused to give up hope. God heard and answered the prayer of a childhood bride. The doctors were absolutely amazed, and God got the glory for a life that was now healed and whole. Paul was a walking miracle.

What an honor for me that day to get to reconnect with both of them years later. Their love had blossomed and deepened over time. Suffering has a way of doing that. Their son Johnathan is a star player on the team and leads in quarterback sacks. His nickname? The Exterminator. Their younger son David was the ball boy, as he ran back and forth on the field, supplying the teams with dry footballs. I watched their eyes as they would lovingly follow his movement. Once in a while, he would look up in the stands, and wave at his parents. They would respond with a shout of, "Good job, David!" Paul informed me that Johnathan had injured his shoulder in the last game, and was in a lot of pain. The coach had made him sit out this game on the sidelines. "Doctor's orders." Paul said.

We had a great time cheering on our team together. We yelled and hollered and jumped up and down like fans do. I watched my grandson throw some amazing passes to help lead his team to a 50-0 victory. They crushed their opponent. I felt bad for the other team and was secretly cheering them on too. At one point, Paul left for a few minutes and then returned to the stands, beaming. "I just talked to the coach," he said "and my son can play in the next game." It was only three days away. "But how can that be?" I asked him, "I thought he was hurt and in a lot of pain." He looked at me and said, "Pain won't stop him." I just smiled. I understood. He was his father's son. A definite chip off the old block. He was a fighter like his dad.

I was overwhelmed with how deep the love of God is for His children. I left that stadium with a renewed sense of gratefulness in my heart for God's faithfulness. I thanked the Lord for giving me the best seat in the house that day. God had reserved it just for me. It was 'The Glory Seat.'

Fall is More Than Just a Season

Patty Knox

James 3:2 We all stumble in many ways.

What comes to your mind when you hear the word 'Fall?' Fluttering gold and red leaves above your head when you are out on a leisurely stroll? Perhaps you think of ripened corn stalks, pumpkins on the vine, apple cider, children back in school and all the other quaint reminders that fall is in the air.

When I think of fall, I think of tripping, flailing arms and legs, unintentional summersaults, and finding one's body flat on its back! I have developed such a habit of stumbling and falling that I can drop on command like a Schnauzer seeking a snack. My body has become so accustomed to tripping that it now bypasses my mind before it can signal me a "look out" and instead pummels me straight to the ground.

While I'm on this subject, I want you to know also that my body does not discriminate where it deposits me, or even when. It gives me zero warning whatsoever and shows no sense of embarrassment or shame when it decides to recline. It has tried to bed down in the church parking lot, the store aisle, up stairs, down stairs, inside and outside. You name it and I have most likely stumbled over it, around it, under it or on top of it.

Just this last Christmas I was decorating the chair rail that leads to our upstairs and soon found my body heading into drop and roll mode, but this time I was ready to fight back and after the second rollover I somehow was able to turn my body into the wall and pull out of it. I stood to my feet determined to continue the decorating and didn't even asses the damage until I had finished! A couple bruises and half a limp is all I came away with.

I didn't fare so well at the grocery store though. I went down flat on my back in the dairy aisle which happens to have the most incoming traffic. When my mind realized the ridiculousness of my body on the cement floor with not only a shopping cart over me but also shoppers looking me over, I was tempted to fake a fainting episode and just keep my eyes closed until the strong handsome firemen carried me out on a stretcher.

Now, I would have been embarrassed had it not been for the expressions on bystanders faces all experiencing embarrassment for me, so instead I settled for humiliation! Where, I ask you, are the dairy workers during these unfavorable circumstances? Why are they not out directing aisle traffic? "Okay folks keep moving toward the meat section, there is nothing to see here."

An elderly woman looked on with eyes wide and face aghast which seemed to literally freeze in that expression. An elderly gentlemen offered his services but by the size and frailty of his frame I knew if he tried he would soon be on the floor next to me. I would have attempted the "pick yourself up by the boot straps" thing, but since I wasn't wearing boots and am not really sure what it even means I instead opted to stand to my feet and pretend like it was just an ordinary event (little did they know it usually is). The spectators pretended back, just like they pretended not to stare and life in the supermarket resumed. Traffic headed off to their designated directions while I hotfooted it down the first available aisle that led to an exit!

My falls have become so public now that I am considering starting my own holiday "Bite The Dust day" where I can feel free to stumble, tumble and yes even trip and turn my ankle without shame.

I am sure glad that God doesn't shame or humiliate us when we trip and fall, aren't you? And I am really comforted by the scripture that tells us that a righteous man may fall down seven times but he gets up again. The number seven in the bible refers to completion. Not that we won't stumble again, because we will, but because Jesus promises to always help us back up on our feet and even complete the store aisle journey with us, or any other place we may find ourselves stumbling or biting the dust in. This truly brings me great encouragement.

What about you? Do you find emotionally or spiritually that it is hard to get up once you have fallen or been pushed down by someone else's careless words or actions? Perhaps you yourself made a bad choice that tripped you up and made you fall flat on your face? Have you felt the sting of embarrassment and humiliation that makes you want to stay down for the count and just lay low? I know I have many times. But I have also learned a valuable lesson from my 'fall' experiences and it is this. The good Lord above does not focus on the many times we may fall but waits close by in eager anticipation for us to call out to Him so He can gently help us up, tend to our wounds, restore our dignity and speak to us with solid assurance that falling down does not count us out.

Isn't this great news? So the next time you feel counted out, when you get to number seven pick yourself up by the bra straps (or boots if you so choose), and keep walking knowing Jesus is walking close beside you and that your heavenly father's mercies are new every morning! Having said all that I believe I'll head to the store.

The Redeemed Lawnmower

Margie McCready

Psalm 103:4 Who redeems your life from the pit, and crowns you with love and compassion.

It was a warm spring morning. I stepped out into the sunlight. I love the outdoors. I love to garden. I love my yard and all my flowers. I love nice green grass and I love to mow the lawn. But this morning, all of that would have to wait. This was a day for cleaning out the garage. It is never a fun task but it is a necessary one. My husband Mark and I are extreme opposites so any endeavor we tackle together is a challenge. I like to be methodical and scrutinize everything. All he can think about is the next coffee break and what we're eating for lunch. As he wheeled out our green lawnmower, I looked at it and smiled. 'Old Faithful' I called it. We had owned this mower for twenty years. We had bought it brand new from Sears. It was a beauty brand new, but years of use had taken its toll.

In reality, Old Faithful was no longer doing the job. We both agreed it was time to purchase a new one. I felt sad. That lawn mower was like a friend to me. Many times when I felt stressed, I would go outside and cut the lawn, even when it didn't need to be mowed. It was therapy for me. I did some of my best thinking when I was cutting the lawn. When my life felt like it was spinning out of control, it was something that I felt I could control.

"We can't throw it away." I said to Mark. I couldn't bear the thought. Our town has a little store named Waste-Not-Want-Not, they take everything you no longer want and either sell it or recycle it. I helped Mark load the lawnmower in the back of the truck and watched him drive off. The lawnmower looked lonely to me and I felt a twinge of loss.

A week later we priced new mowers and were shocked at how expensive they were. Mark decided to look for a used one on our local website, 'Jefferson Buy, Sell, or Trade.' Sure enough, in our neighboring town, only 15 minutes away, a man was selling two used mowers. They were both priced at $80 each. Upon talking to the man, Mark realized he was a fellow Christian we went to church with back in the 80's. "Come on by!" he said to Mark, "You'll be happy with either one!"

As my husband pulled up in Dan's driveway, he noticed the garage door opened and the lawn mowers sitting side by side. Our old friend came out his front door grinning from ear to ear so happy to see Mark after all these years. As Mark scanned the mowers, he couldn't believe his eyes! He would know that mower anywhere! Even with the new wheels! Mark looked up at Dan, "That's my mower!" He said. He then explained to Dan that he had dropped it off at Waste-Not-Want-Not the week before. Dan said, "When I woke up one day last week, it was sitting in my yard. My best friend owns Waste-Not-Want-Not, and he saves the mowers for me. I fix them up and resell them to make some extra money on the side. I put on some new wheels, fixed the automatic choke, put in a new spark plug, put on a new pull string and a new handle and tuned her up. Then I washed her real good. She looks like new. And since you were the original owner, you can have her for $60! And I would say that's a real steal."

I heard Mark pull up in the driveway. I was excited to see if he picked up a new mower. I couldn't believe my eyes! All spiffed up and sitting in our driveway was Old Faithful! I was speechless. She had been redeemed. Bought back. Exactly what Jesus Christ did for us. All of us were sitting in the junk pile and the

Lord said, 'that one's mine. I'll pay the price. That one belongs to me.' We are redeemed. We paid a measly $60 to redeem what was ours. Jesus paid with his life. The highest price anyone could pay.

Amazing grace.

The Car with the Glitch

Margie McCready

Glitch – A defect, error, or malfunction as in a machine or plan.

We were in the market for a different car. With five children, and a couple extra with us most of the time, we needed something a little larger than what we currently owned; A beautiful station wagon purchased just months ago. It seemed like a great deal at the time, but the money we were spending on gas was killing us. You could literally see the needle moving as you were driving down the road. Unfortunately our children loved this car! Breaking the news to them was not going to be easy. My husband and I sat them down, "We have a decision to make." I explained. "We can either eat or put gas in the car." It was a no-brainer, the ultimatum worked splendidly! They all ran into the kitchen and found something to eat while dad took the car back.

The search for a new car was on, but in the meantime, we borrowed a car from my dad. It was an old blue Chevrolet, one that had been sitting out in his field for a few years. My mom had driven the wheels off it. And like an old horse that had seen better days, it was put out to pasture. The good news is that it still ran. "The engine is just fine." My dad had said. But what he had failed to mention, is my mom had hit something pretty hard and it completely bent the frame. Mark and I knew we were not in a position to be picky, so off we drove in the car that was getting a second chance. It was a nightmare. Not only was the inside of this car moldy and the smell was horrible, this car appeared to be going sideways down the road. It was an optical illusion, of course, but you never really felt like you were staying on your side of the road. It was humiliating, and our kids were horrified. "It is only for a short time." I told them, but they chose to walk most of the time. Our gas bill went down very quickly.

In six months, we had saved up enough money to purchase a different car. We found a dark gray 1987 Ford Taurus at a dealership in our town and boy, was it a beauty. During the test drive, my husband and I thought we heard a little knock coming from the engine. We mentioned our concern to the dealer, who quickly assured us that the noise was nothing at all. "This car purrs like a kitten," He said, "it was just a little glitch." I remember thinking, 'Is that all? Who cares about a little glitch?' Well, we should have looked up the word 'glitch' in the dictionary before we signed on the dotted line. Webster clearly defines it as: a defect, error, or malfunction. To put it bluntly, we bought a lemon, a big fat lemon.

A few months after we bought the car, it began stalling. That is not so good when you're the first one at a stoplight. One day we were actually sitting at a stoplight waiting for it to turn green. When it did, we proceeded to move forward only to hear the noise of what sounded like a jet crashing. I was horrified. "What was that?!" I asked Mark. He looked in his rearview mirror. "I think our engine is lying on the road." He calmly said. "That is impossible!" I yelled, "Engines don't just drop out of cars!" Boy, was I wrong, this one did. And it actually happened twice; a year later when Mark was on a business trip driving through Olympia. He gave the car away to a mechanic who wanted it for the parts.

As I think back over our unpleasant car experiences, I can see a spiritual lesson for my own life. There were times where the pressures of life stalled my spiritual engine. There were a few times when I needed a major overhaul, my spiritual engine had dropped out and where could I go but to the Lord? He is always faithful and ready to help us and to restore us. Unlike cars, He will never put us out to pasture, He gives us a new engine (heart) and keeps us moving in the right direction, if we will just keep our hand in His.

I Need to Make a Return

Jennifer Knox

2 Chronicles 30:9 The Lord your God is gracious and compassionate. He will not turn his face from you if you return to him.

My husband has put up with a lot of my "good ideas" in the past, but few have measured up to one I had early on in our marriage. Several years prior, I had taken a class in college that focused on customer relations. One of the primary examples I remember our professor using was that of Nordstrom. He raved about their customer service and said they had one of the best reputations in the nation; due in large part to their return policy. He said hands down, Nordstrom was the best when it came to returning items to their store.

This played heavily into my "great suggestion" to my husband in our first year of marriage. College was still fresh in my mind when we received a large bag of clothes from my husband's uncle. Inside the bag we found a treasure trove of clothing: shirts, pants, jackets, you name it, and it was in there. To a poor newlywed couple this was like winning the lottery! It was even more exciting when we saw that all the clothes were from none other than "the greatest return store of all time"… Nordstrom!

My husband quickly tried on all the clothing, only to discover that it was all too big for him. That was when my four years of education came into full use. I told him what my wise professor had told us about Nordstrom's return policy and how we could take the clothes back and exchange them for sizes that would fit. We scooped up the pile of clothes, shoved them into a bag and headed off to make our return.

The store attendants were more than a little surprised when we handed over the obscenely large bag of clothes and asked to return them for a different size. They scurried off into a corner to discuss the matter with other associates and then with the manager. All the while I looked through racks of clothes finding sizes that would fit my man.

My husband and I were both a little caught off guard when the manager came bearing our bag of clothes and informed us that he couldn't accept our return. He gently pulled out a pair of pants and pointed to the Nordstrom label inside. "You see this label?" he asked us. "Yes," we replied. He continued, "Well… Nordstrom hasn't used this label in over ten years." He went on to show us a new pair of pants sporting the updated label. "On top of that," he graciously continued, "these clothes have been worn and altered and so can't be returned."

I was horrified! I knew my husband was dying, but I tried to play it cool since the whole thing had been my idea! I calmly took the bag of clothes back from him and nonchalantly looked over other shirts and pants for sale (trying to fool them into believing I might make a purchase… although I had no money). As we were heading out of the store, I looked down at our oversized load of ten year old clothing and noticed the bag we had chosen to place all the clothes in. It was from our local thrift store shop! In big bold letters across the bag it read, "VALUE VILLAGE!" I knew there was no playing off my error, so I tried to convince my husband that it was no big deal that we had just entered Nordstrom with an oversized Value Village bag containing ten year old, altered clothing.

To say the least, we weren't able to make a return, but it did make me think about a passage in the Bible. 2 Chronicles 30:9 says, "The Lord your God is gracious and compassionate. He will not turn his face from you if you return to him." What an amazing God we serve! When we have fallen flat on our faces into a mess of sin, we can always return to Him and He will accept us back. I love that it says, "He will not turn His face from you." I thought back to the sales clerks turning away from us, no doubt having a great laugh, but it isn't that way with the Lord. He is quick to forgive and accept us back, and that is good news for a girl who has had to make many "returns" back to the Lord!

Zoo Doo

Patty Knox

Genesis 1:25 God made the wild animals according to their kind …and God saw that it was good.

Believe it or not, I have been given a chance to be in a Zoo Doo lottery, better known as a fecal festival at our local zoo in Seattle. All during the year, workers at the Woodland Park Zoo shovel the doo from the Elephants, Rhinos and Giraffes and make it in to the best compost around. Believe me when I say that it has become so popular, one now has to enter a lottery to get the stuff.

A lottery for zoo dung and I entered (tad bit shocked myself)! I actually felt my competitive side coming out when I entered the contest via e mail this morning. I was envisioning my plants "tall" thanks to the giraffes' contribution, and "huge" thanks to the elephants' deposit and lastly "sturdy" plants due to the accounts payable from the rhinos' stockpile of Zoo Doo.

Now, I haven't told my hubby yet that I entered us into the drawing because I probably won't be chosen due to the popularity of the goods, and the fact that he would roll his eyes and blurt out "You did what?" I don't expect him to understand the value of Zoo Doo and its effect on my flowers and veggies. He wouldn't understand until I presented him with a tomato the size of a basketball, or a corn stalk that stood over nine feet tall. The proof is in the pudding, the rich nutritious Zoo doo pudding!

I mean think about it here, a bazillion folks fight traffic to go downtown to sports events, do they not? Or, venture to Seattle to catch a show at the Fifth Avenue Theatre or simply wander down to see the famous flying fish at the Pike Place Market. So why should one be rattled if they have to fight traffic for something that they can at least bring home as a souvenir (I say this for ammunition just in case my name is chosen).

I fully understand the hassle of securing the truck load of Zoo doo so one doesn't get a ticket, plus the high probability that the stench will temporarily fill up the freeway or that one may himself become a stench to fellow drivers as you whiz by and the cover from the back of the truck lifts and flaps in the breeze. However, frowns and pinched noses are a small price to pay for such a big benefit in my estimation.

Who would have guessed that when God finished creating the wild animals and said it was good, part of that good was fertilizer. I think we have all heard the quote claiming the grass is always greener on the other side of the fence and now I'm thinking it is because some lucky lottery winner got a hold of some Zoo doo!

This whole Zoo doo lottery got me to thinking of something else too. Could it be when the bible talks about all things working together for our good, that all the refuse that comes our way, the good Lord can and will recycle into spiritual compost that will help us grow into healthy, strong Christians? Can it be that the muck we find ourselves sloshing around in, be it from our own misguided steps or someone else throwing it under our feet, have the potential to benefit us by developing our character? And what about the doo doo that hits the fan and then gets aimed right in our direction splattering us from head to toe? Could these experiences make us solid and stalwart in our faith? I think maybe these questions could help shed some light on what the bible calls trials, testings and troubles.

In Romans chapter five of the New Testament, Paul tells us to rejoice in our suffering, because we know that it produces perseverance. This word means to put up with a hardship, to endure, hang tough, withstand, stick it out (plug the nose), and perseverance leads to character, or the level of good standing that leads to hope. James, just a few books forward in the Bible amens Paul's words by declaring a few of his own in chapter one where he exhorts us to consider it pure joy (intense happiness) whenever we face trials of many kinds because the testing of our faith works to make us mature, complete and lacking nothing!

Well, there you have it! We become mature through manure! Who knew that the stink we find ourselves in from time to time could be considered good for us and have a purpose that produces positive effects in our lives?

I would suggest that the next time a shovel of compost comes our way that instead of throwing it back or turning the fan, we welcome it joyfully and allow the Holy Spirit's fertilizer to do the work in our hearts that it was intended to do.

After all, imagine having your hope increase to its highest position and being able to see clearly in all directions like the Giraffe, or as strong in your faith as the Rhino is in muscles, not to mention having spiritual ears as large as the elephant's to hear the Spirit loud and clear when He beckons us. No wonder when God created the wild animals He said it was good. It was good for all of us, man and beast (fertilizer included)!

Burned

Jennifer Knox

Psalms 147:3 He heals the brokenhearted and binds up their wounds.

I've never liked motorcycles. To me it seems beyond comprehension how they allow such things on the road! If you just stop and think about it for a moment, I think you will agree with me. When you go to purchase a car would you ever consider one without seat belts? How about no airbags? Or one that has absolutely no siding at all? There is a name for such a vehicle... motorcycle!

As much as I've voiced my opinions over the years of my utter disdain of "the beast," my husband loves them! So, eventually the inevitable happened and we became the owners of a motorcycle. On the day my husband drove it home he was eager to take our entire family on a test ride. I talked to my kids about safety and the importance of wearing a helmet, holding on tight, and wearing long pants. The salesman at the dealership informed us of the dangers of bare legs touching the tailpipe. "One touch to the tailpipe and you will have a major burn!" the clerk informed us.

I kissed each of my kids good-bye as I sent them off on "the beast" to face the open road with no seat belt, no air bag, and no metal siding to keep them safe. Now mind you, they never left our cul-de-sac! I watched as my husband drove each child safely around our cul-de-sac and back up our driveway. I must admit, I had a sigh of relief as each one returned safely to me. Then the unexpected happened! My husband asked if I would take a spin around the cul-de-sac with him! Me? On "the beast?" There was really no escaping, I was going to take a ride.

I strapped on the helmet, looked for a seat belt (there was none) and then threw my leg over the top of the seat. There was just one tiny problem, I had forgotten my own rule about wearing pants. It was summertime and I had on a pair of capri pants. The very moment I flung my leg over that motorcycle, my leg hit the side of the blazing hot tailpipe. Natural reaction took over and I yanked my leg off that thing faster than you could blink, but the damage had already been done.

I didn't mention anything until I took my thirty-five second jaunt around the cul-de-sac. When I got off and inspected my leg, there was a bright pink burn on my inner calf. I put some cold water on it and tried to control the pain. Two days of me limping around the house passed until I knew I had to go to the doctor. (Actually, my friend told me I was going to lose my leg to gangrene if I didn't get it looked at. That scared me into going.)

When the doctor came in to see my leg he immediately said, "Motorcycle burn! They all look the same, egg shaped burn on the inner calf. This burn has gone all the way through the muscle." It kind of made me sick to hear, but was surprised he knew his burns so well. He gave me a shot, scraped off the dead skin, put some ointment on it and wrapped it up.

By the time I was hobbling out of the doctor's office the pain was so sever that I could barely put any pressure on my leg. I kept it elevated for several days just to control the pain. As I was laying there with my bandaged calf I committed to never getting on a motorcycle again! I didn't even think they were safe to begin with, and here I was with a burned leg!

The whole thing got me thinking about how many times in my life I had been "burned" by a painful event and swore never to let it happen again.

Many people get hurt by others in a church, and then swear never to step foot in a church again. Or a spouse is betrayed by their partner and they close their heart off to anyone who could hurt them again. Or a child who is hurt by a parent. The list is endless. We have all been hurt by someone in our life and we are left to suffer as the wound is healing. Many of us will have wounds that seem to never heal. Days turn into months, months turn into years and still the pain is crippling. I've known this kind of pain myself.

There was one verse that I held on to during my darkest, most painful days. It's the verse found in Psalms 43:18 "The Lord is close to the brokenhearted." I thought about how I felt when one of my four children were sick. I love all my children the same, but when one of them is sick, that is the one who has my full attention. How much more does God feel concern and love for us when we are hurting? On those long and painful nights as I laid crying into my pillow I knew that my God was sitting right there with me... I had His full attention.

As much as my heartache has made me want to close off from people, and keep from risking being hurt, I know that God's way is better. He says in Psalms 147:3 that "He heals the brokenhearted and binds up their wounds." If we allow Him, He will bind up our wounds. And once healed… we are ready to get on the motorcycle of life again! (Well… maybe not a motorcycle, but maybe a nice, big, safe SUV!)

Ornery Old Ma Hyde

Patty Knox

Mark 12:31 Love your neighbor as yourself

Understanding people and maintaining healthy relationships with them in some instances, can be easy, plus quite enjoyable and rewarding. These folks have sunny dispositions, pleasant personalities and are easy to have conversations with. These neighbors are easy to love.

But other people who we find ourselves surrounded by can make it exceptionally difficult to like, let alone love. And make no mistake we will all encounter these cantankerous ones at some stage in our lives. And if we are brutally honest with ourselves we will admit that people have and will bump into us from time to time also. This group can be abrupt, not to mention difficult. They seem to derive pleasure from making things unpleasant, unfulfilling, and very unrewarding for others around them. That's how I first viewed ornery old Ma Hyde when I was around ten years old, and she was around ancient.

I got my first glimpse of the stout little German woman when we pulled into Aunt Leona's driveway, whom I had come to visit with for a few days. In fact, when any of my mother's sisters came by I was always up for a visit. I guess getting out of Dodge even if it was just a couple miles up the street was enough to separate myself from my eight siblings for a bit and receive my Aunts' royal treatment now that their kids were grown and had flown the coop.

I did enjoy being with my siblings however, and always started missing them on the first evening of my visits, but I plowed through knowing that ice cream, soda pop and candy of all kinds awaited me if I stuck it out. The thoughts of eating it all myself made it worth the waves of homesickness that ebbed and flowed until I fell asleep.

Stopping at the end of Aunt Leona's driveway on this particular day, I noticed the door of her rental home next door was opened just enough for me to see a short, portly woman with braids that seemed to wrap around her head numerous times while her face sported the biggest frown I had ever seen on an ancient human face. Then the door suddenly slammed shut. Aunt Leona assured me that her neighbor ornery

Ma Hyde had a bark much bigger than her bite. But I soon had second, not to mention third, thoughts on that statement each time me and Aunt Leona headed out her back door.

That's when the ruckus always started. Ornery Ma would stomp out onto her front porch and give my aunt the... well, let's just say that it was not the royal treatment like I was being given. There was no "howdy neighbor" greeting either. Why, ornery old Ma Hyde didn't seem to agree with my Aunt Leona on anything and told her so with new adjectives every time a subject was changed. It didn't stop there either! Gracious sakes no, why ornery Ma even heckled Auntie all the way to the clothesline and back. I was convinced my Aunt had nerves of steel as she always seemed to be able to turn a deaf ear, stay calm and go on about her business, but not me. If truth be told here, my nerves were frayed and short circuiting because ornery Ma Hyde scared the heebie jeebies out of me! She not only sounded mean, but looked the part too. In fact, Ma Hyde was the stuff nightmares are made of, you know where the boogie man chases the kid in slow motion, but in this nightmare it was the boogie woman.

She was maybe only a few inches taller than myself but I had the feeling her bite could take you out with one chomp. And if that failed, she could lasso you with that ten foot braid looped around her head and drag you for miles before she tired out! Somebody needed to move and it was not about to be my dear Aunt Leona!

That evening at dinner I suggested evicting ornery Ma Hyde. After all, the only thing they seemed to have in common was their last name. This is when Aunt Leona dropped a bomb that sent my frayed nerves in every direction. She informed me that this was not a suitable option since Ma Hyde was her mother-in-law! Family? Was I somehow related to ornery Ma Hyde too? Should I pack my bag and get out now while I can? After all, what good is candy and ice cream if you have your teeth knocked out and a fat lip, I ask?

But I didn't go home and the next day I marched over to ornery Ma's front porch. Why? I don't remember my logic at the time, maybe I was going to evict her myself. But I remember trembling as I knocked gently on her door thinking maybe this was a bad idea after all and she wouldn't hear. She must have seen me coming because she instantly jerked the door open. As Ma looked at me I saw a flicker of tenderness. Then she did something that I was not at all prepared for. She invited me in! Oh dear, was this a trap, would she hold me hostage just to annoy Aunt Leona? But before I realized what I was doing, I stepped inside. Ma pointed me toward an old rocker that sat opposite hers. I don't know what happened then to make Ma Hyde open up and share her pain with me that day. Maybe it was because I was the first visitor in a long, long time. Or perhaps because I was a child and wouldn't try to give advice but would just listen, and listen I did, as I sat in that old rocker while Ma emptied her heart. When I left her little home that afternoon, I now knew why Ma was acting so ornery. She was lonely and felt misplaced. It seemed that her life served no purpose. That there was no place for her in the lives of others.

Well, guess who I visited every afternoon for the rest of my stay at Aunt Leona's? Yep, Ma Hyde. Each visit lasted longer as she recalled the good old days. She even made cookies on the last day I visited and that's when I noticed something different about Ma. Her frown had turned upside down. I was truly going to miss our daily visits and now wished Ma Hyde was my neighbor.

Later that week as Aunt Leona's car headed out of the driveway to take me home, I looked toward Ma's house, and caught a glimpse of a sweet little lady with a smile waving in my direction.

I think maybe Aunt Leona figured out what was making Ma so ornery too and made a special effort to include her into more things, because the times following seemed okay between Ma Hyde and Aunt Leona. I know one thing, I never thought of calling Ma ornery anymore, not once I heard her story and listened with my heart. Perhaps this is the start to loving our neighbors as ourselves.

It is definitely an irrefutable fact that our attitude toward people will determine their attitude toward us. I honestly believe the most constructive way to live this life is to love others. Yes, even the "orneriest" among us because when we do, we will see bitterness fade, inferiority will be replaced by self confidence and a deep sense of belonging will surface.

I'm proud to say that Ma Hyde is part of my family. She passed on and lies very close to Aunt Leona's plot now in the little graveyard in my hometown of Quilcene. I visit that resting place from time to time to stand by all of my loved ones who have journeyed on, and I realize as I gaze across all the headstones, that kindness and friendship and love while living is of much more value than an extravagant floral display after one dies.

Oh, that we would seek the Holy Spirit's help to love others as ourselves. Yes, even the so called difficult and ornery because so many lonely and misplaced Ma Hydes are standing with their doors cracked, waiting for a visitor with a listening ear and a neighbor's smile. Is there someone the Lord wants to love through you today?

The Picnic

Margie McCready

Jeremiah 29:11 "For I know the plans I have for you," declares the Lord, "plans to prosper you and not to harm you, plans to give you hope and a future."

It was the summer of 1978. I was living in a little town on the Olympic Peninsula, where I was raised. When I left my hometown as a new bride in 1972, I never dreamed I would ever return there to live. But sometimes life throws you a curveball. I never saw it coming. I was abandoned in the city with 1 year old twin baby girls. I was in absolute shock and completely devastated. After a few weeks, I could barely function. I knew I needed to go home. When I finally called my mom with the painful news, I could barely utter the words. In her comforting voice, she only spoke three words, "Honey, come home." It was exactly what my heart needed to hear. Home for me was acres of land on a dead end street surrounded by water. The river ran directly behind our house and into the bay, where I spent many hours as a child combing the beach land looking for treasures the tide washed in. A little cabin sat close to the bay. It was very secluded and quiet. A gate separated it from the rest of the world. The girls and I moved in. I needed this place to mend my broken heart and heal. It was therapy for me. I needed to be close to my mom again. She had been my lifeline through a very rocky childhood.

After being back home for four years I began to get restless and knew it was time to move on. The Lord was stirring something in my heart, a call to start living again…to trust again. I rededicated my life to the Lord and began attending a little church in Port Townsend; a town 30 miles away. One particular Sunday afternoon, the church was hosting a picnic at Old Fort Townsend State Park. I decided it would be good for me to branch out and I knew Melanie and Rachel would love playing with the other children. I sewed them each a new outfit, Rachel's was red and Melanie's was blue. I often dressed them in those two colors so my family members could tell them apart, since they were so identical in their looks. They were the joy of my life.

I was helping set up the picnic tables when I noticed a motorcycle coming down the hill towards us. There was a huge watermelon strapped to the back. Curious as to whom it was, I watched as he pulled up and removed his helmet. I was completely caught off guard. He was tall, dark, and very handsome. I instantly blushed and looked away. My first thought was, 'Where has this guy been hiding? I've never seen him in church before.' I couldn't help but notice every move he made. He was outgoing, very friendly, and had a charismatic personality. When it came time to get in a circle and give thanks for the meal, he positioned himself next to me. Everyone joined hands! I felt light-headed when he grabbed my hand. He held it very tenderly, and not at all like he was supposed to. I was so offended! This man was way too fresh. I avoided him the rest of the day.

I didn't see him again for two months, but I dreamt about him every night. I made a decision with winter approaching to move to Port Townsend. I loved my little church and I wanted to be closer to all the friends I had made. I chose a new apartment complex with a view of the water. I had no idea that it just happened to be the same place my dream man was living. I was shocked when two weeks later he knocked on my door. He had seen a lady from our church standing on my balcony and was curious as to who was living in apartment #42. When I could finally find my voice, I invited him in for a cup of tea. I didn't even drink tea! Did I even have any? I was completely rattled. We had a wonderful visit and he was very nice and easy to talk to. I loved everything about him. He came over the next night and barbecued us steaks. They were delicious. He was perfect. Too perfect. And only nineteen. I knew I needed to be open and honest with him. I had to tell him that I was looking for a husband. I assumed that would end our visits. I never expected him to come back. In fact, I encouraged him not to. I was secretly falling in love with him. As fate would have it, wild horses couldn't keep him away (I liked to think so anyway).

We were married two months later, and the rest is history.

35 years and counting.

5 beautiful daughters.

11 amazing grandchildren.

A cozy little two story home we raised our girls in, the same home our grandchildren know fondly as 'Granny and Grandpa's.'

We all have a past. Sometimes we suffer with the things that have hurt us and feel paralyzed to move on and live again. Though we can't change what has happened to us, we can learn from our past and find healing. Jesus offers us a beautiful future. He can redeem our past, no matter how painful it may have been. It doesn't matter if we are the ones who messed it up, or if it was someone else, we can be healed and transformed by His tender touch. He makes all things new. That includes us.

Ummm... I'm Seeing Inside My Eye!

Jennifer Knox

Deuteronomy 31:6 Be strong and courageous.
Do not be afraid or terrified because of them,
for the LORD your God goes with you; he will
never leave you nor forsake you.

As I was climbing into bed one day, I was pondering my days of youth. The days when I could pull an all nighter and still have energy to spare by the next evening... those days are long gone! I enjoy going to bed early. I enjoy snuggling down in my blankets. I enjoy putting my earplugs in my ears to block out all nightly distractions. I enjoy blasting my face with my fan on high. I enjoy my pillow. I enjoy the dark... except for when my husband's in bed with his computer on. He is a night owl. I am a morning owl. Is there such a thing? Anyway, on this particular night, I was ready for all lights out when my husband decided to turn on his iPad to catch up on the day's sports highlights. I tried to block out the light of his electronic device (aka: massively bright flashing night light, more akin to a strobe light while one is trying to sleep).

After quite a bit of flipping and flopping, and heavy sighing to show my irritation, I opened one eye ever so slightly to see what it was he was watching at this unheard of hour of the night (at least 10:30 pm)! It was at that moment that the strangest thing started to flash in front of my slightly opened eye. I could see in black and white a massive grouping of rectangular shaped boxes bouncing and bumping around. Between these boxes were squiggles of lines moving about as well. As my husband's iPad flashed to another scene, it would adjust the light reflecting off my pillow (the area I was looking at). When the light would change, the "boxes and squiggles" would disappear and I again was looking at my pillow. If the light held steady, I could again see the bouncing black and white images.

It began to hit me, "I'm seeing the inside of my eye!" I started freaking out... I'M SEEING INSIDE MY EYE! It was like nothing I had ever seen before. I wanted to tell my husband what I was seeing, but I knew he wouldn't believe me when I informed him I could now diagram the inside of my eye! I knew I needed proof of my theory. I immediately jumped out of bed and made my way to the office computer. Then

I did what any true seeker of knowledge would do, I googled "can you see inside your eye?" Sure enough, there were tons of websites, blogs and videos to prove me right. I watched a science video that explained how it happens. Basically, I had the "perfect storm" working for me. The room was dark with a little light, I was staring at a blank object (my pillowcase) and I only had one eye open, and only a tiny bit. With all of those things in place, your eye will actually begin to look for new input. When it can't focus on anything, it begins to look inside itself. (OK, I was a business major, who avoided science classes at all costs, so this in my nonscientific explanation.)

With my proof in hand, I bolted up to my husband and declared my new found knowledge... "I just saw inside my eye!" And just as I suspected, he gave me one of those, "you gotta-be-joking" looks. I was, however, way ahead of the game and shared with him my scientific findings! He was actually impressed! The next few days I tried several times to recreate my experience and see inside my eye, but have only been able to do it one other time. Let me tell you though, for those who can do it... it's amazing!

All this inner eye searching got me thinking about life. It's incredible to think that at any moment our eye could see inside itself, but it is trained to look outside its lens to what's beyond it. The lens is always there, but it never focuses on it… that is, until there is no outside stimulation, and then it begins to search for something to focus on. Isn't that how we can get with the Lord? He is always with us, always loving us, always there to help us, but we often miss Him in the busyness of life. We can get so focused on other things, that we fail to see what is right in front of us. Deuteronomy 31:6 says, "Be strong and courageous. Do not be afraid or terrified because of them, for the LORD your God goes with you; he will never leave you nor forsake you." Maybe today we could all take a moment to turn off the computer, tv, cell phones, radios, and whatever else is distracting us, and just look at the One who stands before us… our loving Heavenly Father.

The Camera

Margie McCready

Judges 17:6 In those days Israel had no king; everyone did as they saw fit.

I glanced at my watch. It was 6:00pm. Where did the day go? I was feeling sad as our weeklong vacation on the Oregon Coast was coming to an end. It was our last night in the beach house we had rented right on the ocean. Our 5 daughters and our grandchildren were with us, as well as my sister Patty, and Mark's brother Kevin. My sister is the life of every party (in this case, vacation), and Kevin is the most adventurous of all of Mark's brothers. He loves the outdoors and has volumes of gorgeous photographs to prove it.

We had decided to walk the seven blocks into downtown Seaside on our last day of vacation and take in the summer festivities. The aquarium was a huge hit with our 10 grandchildren. The vendors were selling little square paper containers that held tiny silver fish that you could feed to the pet seals. We must have purchased 25! The seals would do tricks for these little treats and it was so entertaining to watch! We all came away wet from their antics. Our last stop was the mall that had a carousal the kids wanted to ride. Our grandson Cash lost his first tooth at the carousal. I saw where it had flown after it popped out of his mouth, and the man attending the ride was kind enough to hand it to me, after I managed to get his attention and explain what had happened.

I looked around for my daughter Corinne. It was our turn to make dinner that night, and reluctant as I was to leave the mall, I knew it was time. We strolled the beach on the way home, reminiscing about our week and the wonderful times we shared as a family. Little did we know the nightmare we were about to encounter. We had saved the best for last. I pulled out the beautiful king salmon and halibut and also the fresh cod from the refrigerator. Corinne turned the oven on 400 degrees. We were preparing our fish in the pans for baking when we both noticed a peculiar smell. "What is that smell?" she said, as she looked at me with a puzzled face. "I don't know." I replied, "But it smells like rubber burning. Maybe it's the oven." That is when the nightmare began. As Corinne opened the oven door we were both rendered speechless. Sitting on a pie plate half melted in the oven was a beautiful camera.

Now, there is something you should know about Corinne. She is a professional photographer and has her own business. Her seeing that camera baking in the oven had the same effect on her as when I saw Michael Jackson dangling his baby out of that high rise window. I thought she was going to faint. Her face turned totally white and expressionless. She was frozen. I finally broke the silence. "Who would put a camera in the oven?!" She finally reacted, grabbed the oven mitt, pulled it out of the oven and sat it on the counter. We were both in shock. It was bubbling and smoking and definitely well done. Then came the real horror. Whose camera was this? I remembered Mark had purchased a very nice camera two months earlier that he needed for his job. This camera was black. I couldn't remember if his was black or silver. I also realized my daughter, Heather, had her expensive camera with her, but I was pretty sure hers was sitting on the mantle in the living room. I ran to look and sure enough, it was. There was only one other person that could be the cameras owner, and that was Kevin, Mark's brother. We were convinced it couldn't be his, because he was on a hike that day and he always takes his camera with him. We were as confused as when we first saw the camera in the oven. I told Corinne that I was pretty sure Mark's new camera was silver. We both felt sick.

A few minutes later we heard Kevin's car pull up and the door to the basement opened. I looked at Corinne. "I can't do this." I said. I ran and hid by the refrigerator. I was always the chicken liver of the family. Corinne had placed the camera off to the side of the counter, out of sight. "Hi Kevin." I heard her nervously say. "Did you have a nice hike?" I'm sure her tongue was in 1000 knots. "It was great!" He said. "Did you get a lot of nice pictures?" "No, I didn't take my camera. I dropped my camera in the water yesterday and Mark was drying it out in the oven for me. It's a trick he learned when he had dropped his cell phone in the water." I decided to come out of my hiding place. After all, it wasn't me who turned on the oven. Corinne looked like the cat that was caught with a bird in its mouth. She grabbed the pie plate and held it up to Kevin. "We cooked your camera." His response was none other than shocking. He tipped his head back and started laughing. He kept laughing! I didn't know what to think. Did he have sunstroke? He then went on to explain that the camera was on its last leg. It hadn't been working correctly for months. In fact, he was planning on buying a new one at

Costco the very next day, as it was his birthday and he was treating himself to a brand new camera. The color began to come back into Corinne's face. She was so relieved.

We continued to cook our fish and everyone said it was delicious. Except for Mark. He had burnt camera for dinner, I think he is still picking out the bones.

Parable of the Shopping Cart Wheels

Patty Knox

Ezekiel 10:10 As for their appearance, the four of them looked alike; each was like a wheel intersecting a wheel.

Ever have one of those days when even a short jaunt to the grocery store can seem like an impossible task? In fact, just the mere thought of it sets your nerves, not to mention your teeth on edge? Well, I had one of those days recently, when dinner guests were soon to arrive and to my dismay, I realized I was missing one of the key ingredients to my main entree. Now in my befuddled state of mind I still had enough sense not to send my better half to the supermarket to retrieve the missing items. Why not send Hubby? Because Bob holds the supermarket track record for purchasing unheard of brands with unheard of ingredients that I had no idea existed on store shelves. Please don't get me wrong, I'm married to a wonderful man of God, who when it comes to spiritual food picks only the best top quality grub. And for this I am thankful, however, food containers with unheard of brands and contents is not on my list of wise food choices.

So, grabbing my purse and keys I quickly made a mad dash to the grocery store. Pulling into the parking lot I began praying earnestly (okay, desperately) for a spot up front. Not only was this prayer hindered, but I realized darting in and out of vehicles from the back lot, that in my haste I had forgotten my jacket and wouldn't you know it, a Seattle rain cloud descended on me and had the nerve to stalk me all the way to the front entrance!

Once inside, I quickly scooped up a basket and headed left, thankful that at least I would be spared the traffic jam that occurs when you snag a cart and head to the right. Now I don't know how your supermarket is set up but I'm still scratching my head as to why on earth our bread aisle is just inside the door and due right. This theory makes no sense whatsoever to me. Carts get instantly tangled up. Why? Because bread is a universal necessity. But here's where the problem comes in if you do the equation. If bread is the first item to land in a shopping cart, when unveiled at the checkout stand, it has most likely been reduced to the size and shape of a Swedish pancake. But I think what really burns my toast is being stuck in a bread aisle traffic jam and the store not coughing up some "Smuckers" while I wait for the coast to clear.

So, there I was, basket in tow locating and then quickly apprehending the few items necessary for my dinner and somewhere between a fast trot and a slow gallop I made a beeline to the checkout stand with the sign posted above TEN ITEMS OR LESS. Okay, here's something else that curdles my milk - do these aisles really exist? I'm not convinced, as shoppers always manage to hide little items underneath larger items. Like the lady that was in line ahead of me. When she pried the toilet paper from her basket with brute force, twenty more items sprang up from the bottom. Of course I was in no place to judge as I have been guilty of food smuggling myself on a few occasions.

So here I stood waiting impatiently in line. Not wanting to breeze the covers of the magazines that were staring me in the face (besides they were the same ones from last week), I opted instead to people watch. Something that even in my hurried moments fascinates me. I went from watching folks, to watching what was in their grocery carts. My final focus took me to the shopping cart wheels themselves. I was suddenly struck with the realization that our Christian walk can be very similar to the carts we choose. Now before you stick me on the aisle with the rest of the nuts, let me try to explain.

I can't speak for the shopping carts at your store, but believe me when I say that at my supermarket they are as different as night and day. Or should I say gravy and pudding? What makes them so opposite? IT'S ALL IN THE WHEELS....Oh, granted, these shopping cart wheels all look the same, but this is where the deception of these four little rubber circles come into play. The very moment I set these wheels in motion is the moment I experience either P.S.P. (pure shopping pleasure) or S.C.W.D. (shopping cart wheel disorder).

Honestly now, haven't we all grabbed a cart and soon realize its wheels want to take us every which way but the right way? I call this the sidetracked cart. If I move toward the soup aisle, it wants to lead me down the cookie aisle. If I'm determined to go straight to the vegetables, these distracting rubber feet gravitate toward the ice cream freezer section. I move up the organic aisle only to be routed into the junk food section, and by the time I reach the checkout aisle my plans for eating healthier are placed on hold, all because of that sidetracked shopping cart encounter.

I find it interesting that our spiritual lives can be very similar to this particular cart we set our sights on on our eternal destiny, only to encounter life's determined distractions. We have noble intentions toward prayer and reading the word, yet life's daily diversions move us in the opposite direction. Yes, our wheels are always in constant motion, however, the question remains are we moving in the direction of our call and purpose or are we like the sidetracked cart going every which way but the right way? Little food for thought, huh?

The next contraption that I would like to introduce is the Spinning wheel cart. Now this little Princess promises to take you to your grocery aisle destination but soon falls short of moving in any direction, because when you set these royal wheels into motion, they begin to spin rapidly in circles, yet to your dismay you soon discover two of the wheels aren't even making contact with the floor. This cart's sick torment is the nowhere fast kind of torture it likes to inflict on the shopper who is in a hurry.

Ever felt like your life fits this description? I sure have. It's like being caught in a whirlwind, spinning in circles and going nowhere. Similar also to a car engine. We can rev the engine all we want but until we shift into drive, we're just commotion without motion. The Lord has equipped us all with spiritual wheels that were meant to engage and move us toward good works and serving others. Spinning in circles makes me dizzy. With the help of the Holy Spirit I'm determined to shift into drive and get moving.......

Then there is the unbalanced cart. It has one wheel that is higher than the others and is tipsy. Even strategically piling groceries inside and over the wheel brings no added relief. You start down the cereal aisle and by the time you are halfway down it, you've clipped several boxes off the shelf, only to look down and see Snap Crackle and Pop at your feet and Captain Crunch under your cart. Your experience with this unbalanced critter takes you to one side of the aisle or the other but knows no middle ground. I'm certain many of us can relate to these wheels in the sense that we are forever seeking balance in our busy lives only to find ourselves in one ditch or the other. And discovering our spiritual carts are unbalanced, we attempt to remedy the situation by piling on extra things to fix the problem. But not only do we continue to be out of balance, now we have added extra weight to our lives.

I think the absolute worst kind of shopping madness is the close encounter with the monster of them all. The dreaded BUMPY-SQUEALING CART.

This deceptive duo lets you get half way down the first aisle before it decides to manifest. Then it takes on a rocking motion with hideous obnoxious squeals that emit from its treads. And it never fails that when you land such a cart as this you are in a hurry and don't have time to return it. Before long you sense disdainful glaring faces pressing into the back of your head by fellow shoppers who you know are fighting back strong emotions of aisle rage. You understand their temptation to pelt your bumpy, squealing cart with food from theirs. You continue your decent, bumping and squealing like a pig all the way to the medicine aisle, plucking some Excedrin off the shelf, because you know you will need it for the ride home.

In this life we will experience a bumpy ride from time to time. We'll most likely experience squeaky wheels too, that can have a negative effect on ourselves as well as others. Sometimes we need to stop and listen to where the squeaks are coming from, and then allow the Lord to fix our spiritual carts.

Finally, the last cart I'd like to introduce you to is the shopping cart that graces the title submission. Now this cart lends itself to P. S.P. (or pure shopping pleasure). Its wheels move in complete obedience. These dead to themselves rubber circles seek not their own direction and are not easily side tracked.

They seek not their own aisle destination, and do not offend in bumping or screechy outbursts. Its wheels discern the scripture that man does not live by bread alone and offers Smuckers when rolling by the traffic jams of life. And when at last it wheels into the ten items or less aisle, it is blinded to the faults of others, because it knows the Heavenly store manager will apply His tools to every unbalanced, sidetracked, spinning and bumpy wheel. And that He will carefully apply His oil to every squeak. Then they too, will seek a new direction for their once wayward wheels. The direction that leads to the Heavenly check stand in the sky!

Printed in the United States
By Bookmasters